Child

P

of related interest

Child Welfare Services
Developments in Law, Policy, Practice and Research
Edited by Malcolm Hill and Jane Aldgate
ISBN 1 85302 316 7

Children in Charge
The Child's Right to a Fair Hearing
Edited by Mary John
ISBN 1 85302 368 X

Child Care
Monitoring Practice
Edited by Isobel Freeman and Stuart Montgomery
ISBN 1 85302 005 2

Child Adoption
A Guidebook for Adoptive Parents and their Advisers

R.A.C. Hoksbergen

Jessica Kingsley Publishers
London and Bristol, Pennsylvania

The right of R.A.C. Hoksbergen to be identified as author of this work has been asserted by him in accordance with the Copyright, Designs and Patents Act 1988.

First published in the Netherlands in 1994 as
Een kind adopteren, 3rd edition (ISBN 90 263 1353 5) by
AMBO/Baarn
First published in English in 1997 by
Jessica Kingsley Publishers Ltd
116 Pentonville Road
London N1 9JB, England
and
1900 Frost Road, Suite 101
Bristol, PA 19007, U S A

Copyright © 1997 R.A.C. Hoksbergen

Translation by Saskia Ton, Esther van Velzen
Edited by Henny Corver

Library of Congress Cataloging in Publication Data
Hoksbergen, R.A.C., 1940–
[kind adopteren, English]
Child adoption: a guidebook for adoptive parents and their
advisers / R.A.C. Hoksbergen.
p. cm.
Includes bibliographical references and index.
ISBN 1-85302-415-5
1. Adoptive parents. 2. Adopted children. 3. Adoption.
I. Title.
HV875.H57913 1996
362.7'34–dc20   96-8277
                                                    CIP

British Library Cataloguing in Publication Data
Hoksbergen, R.A.C.
Child Adoption : a guidebook for adoptive parents and
their advisers
1. Adoption
I. Title
362.7'34

ISBN 1-85302-425-5

Printed and Bound in Great Britain by
Cromwell Press, Melksham, Wiltshire

Contents

Dedication

For adoptive parents, 'expecting a child' takes a very special form. This book has been written for these parents. A great deal of attention has been paid to what couples may expect and ample use has been made of the vast amount of research results over the last twenty years.

Adoptive parents are educators who take on a child of different parents. Today that child is most often born in another country. Research and clinical experiences have shown that there are quite a few specific issues adoptive parents of (inter-country) adopted children have to face.

Adoptive parents have a great need to be well prepared for both the medical and psychological problems which may face their children. This book has been written to better prepare both prospective adoptive parents and adoption professionals.

Preface

This book was originally written for parents who wish to adopt a (foreign) child. Therefore a great deal of attention has been paid to what these couples may expect. Ample use has been made of the vast amount of research which has been conducted over the past twenty years.

Throughout these years I have been intensively involved with the phenomenon of adoption. Furthermore, my colleagues and I, working at the Adoption Centre in the Netherlands, are regularly confronted with a variety of, sometimes serious, problems of adoptive children and their parents. It is therefore obvious that adoption centres, social workers and also, especially, the adoptive parents (to be) have a great need for more information about adoption. In this present work, intensive use has been made of the research material and my twenty years experience with my consultation and social practice. This information is reproduced as practicably as possible and is supplemented with practical recommendations.

I gratefully acknowledge the help of many people with the acquisition and incorporation of data. First and foremost, I think of the adoptive parents and adoptive children who were approached for a variety of specific research goals. Several large adoption organisations, in the Netherlands as well as in Belgium, have helped the researchers in a practical sense. Also, many students and staff-members of the Adoption Centre have contributed to its satisfactory progress. To them we owe our gratitude, as well as to Erica Hoksbergen-Evers for her contextual comments and Henny Meerdinkveldboom for her technical support.

CHAPTER 1

What do Adoptive Parents Have to Take into Consideration?

1.1 What is so special about adoptive parenthood?

To many people, having and raising children are among the most important life-tasks. For most of them, having children means a radical change in their lives. It comes with a large sense of responsibility. A child needs two, sometimes three, decades to achieve complete independence and in that time an appeal is made to the educators in various respects. There are educators of various natures. The most common situation is that of a couple who are the fortunate parents of their own biological child or children, conceived naturally. However, there are more ways to become a parent. Since divorce has become more common, step-parenthood has also become more common. I also think of parents of children who have been conceived through artificial means, with or without the use of a donor. Nevertheless, the group which we are especially concerned with here is the group of adoptive parents.

Adoptive parents are educators who find themselves in a very special situation, for they take on a child who always comes from a different family and who, these days, is also often born in a different country. They hope and expect that they will be able to create such a relationship with this child that, on an emotional level, it really becomes 'their child'.

The adoption of foreign foster children has gained a firm foothold in Europe. There are also consequences connected to it. In order to get a better understanding of this, let us first compare a few general aspects of the education situation for biological parents and adoptive parents. With regard to issues such as motivation for parenthood and the number of desired children and education, there can be many differences between biological parents and adoptive parents.

From the very first signs of the child's life, biological parents are involved with his or her development and education. The life-histories of the newcomer, and of the biological parents, are narrowly intertwined from the first moment onwards.

This is different for adoptive parents, who always receive an 'older' child. This 'being older' of the child can mean that it is a baby of only a few weeks or a few months old, but the child can also be five, or six years old, or even older. The integration into the family at an older age can mean that adoptive parents are partially or completely unaware of the life-history of the child. As a rule, very little is known of the pregnancy and the birth, let alone of the biological parents. This applies more to foreign adoptive children than to children who were born in Europe or the United States. Since it is a known fact that, specifically, the first years of the child and the family background (genetic genealogy) are determining factors for the composition and further development of character and personality, it will be clear how different the initial position is for both types of parents.

There is another important difference. Biological parents do not need to ask anyone's consent if they want to have offspring. Having a child is considered an entirely private matter. Adoptive parents, on the other hand, always have to undergo a family investigation first. They are dependent on the judgement of others. An official institution – in the Netherlands, *De Raad der Kinderbescherming* (The Board for Child Protection) and in Belgium, the acknowledged adoption organisations – decides on the suitability of a parental couple to raise a child. As a consequence, aspiring adoptive parents are sometimes turned down. Biological parents, by definition, cannot be turned down a priori. If at a later stage they appear to be less than successful as educators, they can, in the worst case, have their parental duties revoked. With artificial conception, parents likewise need a third party but the demands on these parents cannot be compared to the many demands made on adoptive parents. In a psychological sense there are hardly any demands, even single people are able to have children relatively easy. In so far as demands are made, they mainly relate to the necessary criteria to ensure a medical treatment with as big a chance of success as possible.

A third difference has to do with the legal position. Biological parents will never have to deal with a court of law to which they must posit the question whether they may become the lawful parents of the child. This is an unquestioned and self-evident fact as from the birth of their child. Adoptive parents, after the arrival of their child in the Netherlands, still have to wait an entire year before they are able to apply for official adoption at the court. A report about the past year is prepared by the Board for Child Protection for the court. Only after the judge has signed his approval are adoptive parents (and adoptive children) given the same rights as other parents (and children). In Belgium, and many other countries, the parents of an adoptive child, of whom the adoption certificate has already been signed in the country of origin, need only register the child with the registry office. In the few cases in which this is not so, one is able to apply for the Belgian adoption certificate as soon as the child arrives.

A fourth important difference is the fact that adopting and being adopted have an influence on the raising situation. For biological parents, blood ties play an important part during the process of attachment to their child. The child is theirs as from birth. Adoptive parents will have to get accustomed to the idea that their child, born of strange parents and now come into their lives, really belongs to them. This problem will, to a greater or lesser degree, continue to play a part because as the child grows up he or she will experience their adoption differently. An important task for adoptive parents is to talk to the child about his background and thereby place the biological or birth parents in a neutral or positive light. Sometimes a need for more information, or even contact, develops and this desire may be expressed by either the adoptee or the birth parent (usually the mother). Emotionally these are difficult issues in an adoption family. For non-adoptive parents these problems naturally do not exist.

1.2 The importance of attention to initial problems

There are quite a few specific issues adoptive parents are faced with when the child comes to the family.

First, there can be a variety of medical problems. Sometimes foreign adoptive children come to Europe with specific disease symptoms. Children from (sub)tropical countries still suffer from diseases which have disappeared in our regions (e.g. certain parasitic infections). The children may also show signs of motoric (e.g. walking) and growth retardation. Often these are caused by long-term and serious malnutrition and/or a serious shortage of attention to, and stimulation of, development – in short, by neglect.

These delays in physical development often have a pedagogical-psychological basis. Children who have spent a long period in a children's home have often received too little individual attention and love. It is important for their development and growth to be stimulated in a variety of ways. They should be regularly spoken to, taught to handle toys – no matter how simple – and helped in various ways. A lack of love and stimulation has several negative consequences, as research has made clear. These consequences are summed up by the term 'hospitalism'. The psychologist Rene Spitz first thought of this term immediately after the war. He was confronted by children who, because of the war, were (suddenly) separated from their mother and were taken into, for instance, a home or hospital. The separation from the mother appeared to lead to impairment in mental and physical development. Other effects were: fear of strangers, withdrawal, depressions and a greater susceptibility to diseases and disorders.

Do we also find these medical and psychological problems in adoptive children? Very often we do, as has become clear from extensive research. The most common problems of foreign adoptive children upon arrival, and the first few months afterwards, are: diarrhoea, parasitic infections, susceptibility to infections and retardation in motoric and intellectual development (sitting, walking, talking at a much later stage). Also, on an emotional level, a long-term stay at a children's home often has negative consequences. It can create problems in handling and controlling personal feelings and establishing contact with other children and adults.

We must acknowledge that many children who come from far-away countries or Eastern Europe to Western Europe have had turbulent times. The events which all these children have experienced are not to be wished on any child. The tangible transfer to a Western European country is, as it were, the bridge from a miserable past to a hopeful future.

1.3 A past which causes distress

What did this past often look like?

First, the children were mostly unwanted by either of the parents or the grandparents. This mostly applies to the group of adopted children of unmarried mothers; the many abandoned children and children who were given up at a later age. This unwantedness will be experienced to a greater or lesser degree by small children, especially when the child spends some time with the mother while being emotionally neglected or ill-treated.

This immediately relates to a second indication of the situation. Many children have had a difficult time in an emotional and material sense. The chance of this is greater if the child is older before she is put up for adoption. As a consequence of this neglect, quite a few children are in poor condition. In extreme cases this may result in a child of approximately three years old who is barely able to walk or talk. Depending, of course, on the individual, it is not exceptional for such children to be one or more years behind in motoric and intellectual development.

Many adoptive children have had to deal with different educators. Some children are given up immediately after their birth. Other children first spend some time in the parental home or with relatives. If they end up in a home immediately, there is a great chance that they will have to deal with constantly changing educators. This usually has very harmful consequences for the acquisition of relationships with adults and, therefore, also with future adoptive parents.

Several studies have shown that the bond between child and one or more adults usually develops in the first few years of life. The first obvious signs of attachment of the child to the caring parent can be seen when the child is approximately seven or eight months old. It is possible that the non-committing of a relationship in the early years may lead to what is termed 'the insensitive character'. This is characterised by an initial phase of clinging and dependent behaviour, followed by an attention seeking, unbridled and undifferentiated (everybody's friend) friendliness. Often we see an inability to build lasting relationships and to adhere to various rules. However, the question remains whether it is possible, at a later age, to start relationships which are so strong that the consequences of early negative experiences and disturbances are nullified.

Especially for the group of adoptive parents, the need to answer such questions becomes urgent. They know very little or nothing about the ancestry and the birth parents of the child. Even the information which they do have, for instance, whether the child did or did not live for some time with the birth parents, is usually very vague and impossible to verify. In this aspect they are completely dependent on the willingness of Homes to provide information. And what is more important, they are dependent on the extent to which Homes are at all interested in the ancestry of the child. Frequently only a minimum of details are taken down. A Home often does not have the means to inquire after more information, usually because of the constant lack of money and, thus, lack of staff. Details which may possibly have been collected usually only concern the birth mother of the child. Very seldom is something known about the father. The latter holds for both foreign adoptive children and local adoptive children.

When a child is given up for foreign adoption, he or she will spend some time in a Home – even if it is only for a few weeks or months. This is due to necessary formalities and an observation period to see whether the child complies with the criteria laid down by the receiving countries. After all, not only adoptive parents are subject to a certain selection; the adoptive children are too. The standards do rather vary from country to country. All Dutch and Belgian mediators try to find out as much as possible about the child's state of health. After all, parents should know more or less what to expect when a local institution tentatively proposes a child. This particularly holds for special cases: cleft palate, serious foot disorders, memory disorders, heart disorders and suchlike. However, research and practical cases show that we should not be overly optimistic about the accuracy of the medical reports in the country of origin. This has everything to do with the accuracy with which a child's state of health is seen and checked. Sometimes it is in their best interest not to be too accurate, for example in determining age. After all, the chances of adoption become less when the child is older or has serious medical problems. Still, European countries also appear to be lacking – as may be concluded from a case, known to us, in which a child was diagnosed as having a cleft palate only after a six-month stay with the family and after having been checked by several paediatricians.

1.4 Knowledge about the child's background appears to be very important

We may question the necessity for adoptive parents to have a variety of background information available about their adoptive child. Have they a need for more information than is supplied to them by the different institutions? Are adoptive children themselves interested in hearing or knowing something about their backgrounds?

Several studies have established a link between knowledge of the child's background and the child's more or less successful adjustment. The most striking fact, emphasised by most authors, is that it is the way in which parents deal with the information available to them rather than the amount of information that counts. It appears that when parents have difficulty in answering questions from the adoptive child about its biologial or birth parents, there is usually a less satisfactory relationship between parents and child. The feelings of adoptive parents with regard to the birth parents of the child, and the way in which these are passed on to the child, appear to be very important. Adoptive parents need to talk about the birth parents with as much understanding and respect as possible, answering any questions as openly as possible, when the child is ready. We now know that this openness is very beneficial to a satisfactory family situation. The recognition of the difference between adoptive parenthood and biological parenthood has a positive effect on relationships within the family.

There is also a link between the extent to which the child asks questions about its background and the quality of adjustment. For instance, Jaffee and Fanshel (1970) found that children who insisted on more information, in comparison to those who did not, had more problems with personal and social adjustments, did less well at school, had more problems with heterosexual relationships and, on the whole, showed a more problematic adjustment to life. The adoptive parents of these somewhat more problematic children were less satisfied with the overall adoption procedure.

The results of Jaffee and Fanshel correspond to those of the study by John Triseliotis (1973). In Scotland, where the study took place, it is possible, just as in other European countries, that the adoptee, having reached a certain age (17 in Scotland), is allowed to look at the birth register where the original birth certificate is kept. It is then possible to find out certain details about the birth parents, such as the former address and the name. In Scotland, as in many other countries, it appears that many adoptees make use of this opportunity.

Triseliotis' study deals with 68 adoptees of various ages who inquired about their original birth certificates at the Edinburgh registrar's office. Triseliotis divided these 68 people into two groups: a group of 26 people who only wanted more information about their background and a group of 42 who, in addition to this, wanted to meet their birth parents. These two groups differed greatly from each other. The adoptees who also wanted to meet their birth parents seemed to have three common characteristics in contrast to the other group:

- The adoptive parents had supplied very little or no information about the background of the child. Where they had done so, it was in an awkward and hostile manner with regard to the birth parents.

- The relationship between the adoptive child and its parents was less satisfying.

- The self-image of the adoptee was rather negative.

A similar picture emerges when we look at the results of a follow-up study, completed in 1994, of a group of children from Thailand (Hoksbergen, Juffer and Waardenburg 1986). We first approached this group in 1985, then consisting of 116 children who had been in the Netherlands approximately eight years. Almost ten years later, when we approached them for a second time, the children were almost all in the middle of puberty – a period usually full of storm and stress. Once again there appears to be a link between the way in which the parents deal with the adoption status and their relationship with their child. The parents who, according to the youngsters, had talked little about the adoption had a less pleasing relationship with their adoptive children.

I always call this the first adoption paradox. As the adoptive parents acknowledge the importance of the birth parents and, as it were, involve them in the upbringing, the relationship between the adoptive child and the adoptive parents is strengthened. The adoptee thus experiences a parental sense of respect for his background and his identity. The topic does not have a sense of taboo about it, even though parents may find it difficult to broach it.

The above is a temporary answer to two important questions: if and why it is necessary for adoptive parents to supply information about the child's past, and whether adoptive children themselves are interested. A third question is whether adoptive parents have a need for background information. We have been able to see the importance of this information for adoptive children from the previous section and it is to be hoped that the parents can understand this too. I do, however, have some qualms about this. Too many parents have little interest for more background information. In a study of locally-born adoptive children, about a quarter of the parents said 'rather know nothing' or 'not know too much'. The researchers were struck by the difference between the fathers and the mothers. A majority of the adoptive mothers agreed with the statement 'It's better for adoptive parents to know as little as possible about the background of the child', while the majority of the adoptive fathers did not agree with this.

Let all adoptive mothers and fathers realise, however, that the attitude 'rather know nothing' has an adverse effect on a satisfactory relationship with their child. The result is, what I termed earlier, the first adoption paradox. The more one denies or ignores the existence of the birth parents, the greater the need of many adoptive children to find out more about their background.

For the child herself, her background is essential information. It is also a sign of psychic well-being when the child deals with it. If the adoptive parents show all possible openness (for instance in talking about the country of origin and the biological parents), this will have a positive effect on the trust the adoptive child has for his adoptive parents. The ancestry of the child is the child's property. The more seriously adoptive parents deal with this, the less of a problem it will be for the child. This holds for both his thoughts and fantasies about his origin as well as the influence of this fact on the relationship with his adoptive parents.

1.5 Good preparatory work and a great deal of patience are recommended

Making the decision to adopt a child takes time. Couples who, to their sadness, have had to conclude that they are unable to have children of their own, no matter how hard they try, have to come to terms with their childlessness. Nowadays we also see that the sadness of many failed attempts to become pregnant through *In Vitro Fertilisation* (IVF or test-tube fertilisation) needs to be coped with. This also requires time, and couples must allow themselves that time. Looking forward to an adopted child immediately after the last failed IVF attempt (approximately 15 to 20% of the women treated in this way will eventually give birth to a child) is not to be recommended. The couple must first accept that the desire for children can only be met through adoption, and that an adoptive child is honestly wanted. It is not 'third best': first a biological child, then an AID (Artificial Insemination Using Donors) or IVF child (with or without the use of a donor) and finally an adoptive child.

During this process of deliberation and reconciliation there may be changes in ideas about the adoptive child. One may also discuss it with several other people. I have termed this process 'forethought'. One may assume that adoptive parents not only require a variety of information but also a more contextual insight which may help them to make the right decision for themselves. Proper forethought is in the interest of the adoptive parents. Well-prepared parents are better parents! The following chapters have been constructed with these thoughts in mind.

CHAPTER 2

Why do People Adopt a Child?

2.1 Motives are not easily traced

In psychology, the notion 'motive' has an important place in theories concerning the development of the personality. In short, it is understood to mean the conditions that lie within the person which are needed to come to certain behaviour or thoughts.

The notion 'need' is also essential in connection with this. People have basic needs. For instance the need for warmth and safety, the need for security, the need to give and receive love, the need to be a part of something, sexual needs; needs that some scientists compare with the instincts of animals. Satisfying these needs is considered necessary for the development of the individual. As a counterpart, it holds that obstruction of the satisfaction of these needs leads to stress, and when this obstruction continues it can lead to psychological disorders, sickness and death. As is the case with many psychological concepts, various views exist about why certain needs and motives exist. However, all writers do agree on one thing: the reason why people reach a certain type of behaviour is not easy to trace. Usually it is a mixture of several reasons which are related to one another in a manner which is hard to understand. It is, therefore, impossible to reach ultimate conclusions about the 'why of behaviour' easily. Also, the question as to what extent certain behaviour stems from human nature or results from upbringing, and, therefore, the influence of other people, usually cannot be answered. In psychology this matter is known as the controversy about what is most determining for the development of the human being: nature or nurture.

One should read this chapter bearing the above remarks in mind. I shall try to say some more about people's motives for adopting a child but I do not profess to give the ultimate answer to this question by the end of this chapter. However, for adoptive parents it is of interest to read about how other people have come to the same conclusion. This can be helpful and can encourage them to gain more insight into their own motives for adopting a child and, perhaps, critically examine these motives once more.

In the course of time motives for adoption may change, perhaps due to social trends. It is important for society to realise this. Thus, certain social consequences can be taken into account. Such consequences can be expected anyway; to me it stands to reason that motives for adoption are linked directly to other changes in society. Think about motives for parenthood, views on family structure, the number of children one wants to raise and views on people who give a child away (whether or not they live in the Third World).

2.2 Two groups of adoptive parents

Roughly, I see two very different motives for taking an adoptive child into the family; motives influenced by the actual circumstances experienced by the couple. When you cannot have a child of your own, you will have different views about adoption than when you already have children, or decide not to have any children of your own.

Involuntarily childless couples

First, there is the problem for people who cannot have a child at all, or a second child, or perhaps even a third. People who feel frustrated in their ability to create a family of the desired size and composition. The impediments may be of a diverse variety. Hereditary defects may be a hindrance, while abortion is rejected completely. The man or woman, or both, are infertile and the use of modern fertility-techniques is rejected or one of these techniques has been tried, but without success. In the past few years the latter group has increasingly gained in size among aspirant adoptive parents.

This first and, quantitatively speaking, most important group of adoptive parents mainly consists of married couples who cannot have any children of their own. This applies to the Netherlands, Belgium and other countries. Of all aspirant adoptive parents, approximately 80 per cent are involuntarily childless.

Involuntary childlessness usually involves a constant see-sawing between hope and grief. For many years the couple have been trying to have a child, in several ways and with the use of ever increasing modern aids and resorts. But, time and time again, they have not succeeded. The required sexual intercourse becomes a 'must' and, as such, takes away all the fun. Over the years tension often appears between the couple and sometimes questions of guilt occur.

In relation to this, statistics show that the cause of infertility is equally often due to the man as it is to the woman. Also, there is the group which consists of 10 per cent of all infertile married couples with unexplained infertility. Permanent childlessness as a result of infertility varies between 2.5 and 5 per cent in Western countries (te Velde 1991). In a study of women who were born around 1950, childlessness was caused by infertility in only 2.5 per cent; 4.5 per cent were involuntarily childless for other reasons (among which, infertility in the man) and about 8 per cent were childless by choice! (te Velde 1991).

In most cases, however, there is no question of blame.[1] In such cases one simply has a defect or handicap which is not always explicit. But, as one tries harder and harder to get that one child one exposes oneself to the risk of becoming obsessed with a child-wish. One creates expectations about the great happiness that the child will bring about and hopes that the desire for such wanted motherhood or fatherhood will be fulfilled completely; one will feel more of a man or a woman, form a better relationship with the partner, gain more status in the neighbourhood and family, etc.

Before these people decide to adopt, they would do well to gain a new balance in their needs. They must realise that each child makes its own demands and has a right to develop its individual nature and personality, and that the child is not to be adopted simply to satisfy any needs the parents may have or to solve mutual problems. Aspirant adoptive parents who know the unconscionable grief of the death of a child at birth or, perhaps even worse, the death of a child at a certain age, have an additional problem. Each child, be it a biological or an adopted one, is then at risk of having to go through life as a 'replacement child'. Sometimes, even subconsciously, the child is then expected to fit the image and the memory of the child which has passed away, although a close resemblance can help the parents to get over their grief. Therefore, in Belgium, as well as in the Netherlands, the preparatory meetings of the adoption organisations, or the *Voorbereiding Interlandelijke Adoptie* (VIA), usually deal with the 'necessity of dealing with involuntary childlessness' first. During the family research a lot of attention is paid to this subject as well.

I have briefly said something about the necessity of dealing with the grief caused by the absence of children. But I also have some useful advice to assist with 'coping'. It may prove to be rather important. Let me try. I say this very carefully because I know that with certain couples, sadly enough, this grief will remain dominant. They will remain with an obsession for their entire lives. These people are probably better off not proceeding with an adoption.

Now for some advice:

- ° Consider, together and with friends, whether there are any other fields of life that are valuable to you and which can be sufficiently challenging and satisfying psychologically.

- ° Take your time between the last failed attempt to conceive a baby of your own and the decision to adopt or to become a foster parent. You should use this time to learn about what this form of parenthood is going to mean to you, both by means of conversations and reading material.

---

1   I deliberately say 'most' and not 'all'. In some cases sexual behaviour was of such a nature that it
    led to, for instance, blocked fallopian tubes or other defects.

- This time should also be used to ask yourself why you need this child in your life so badly. Asking yourself this question may lead to seeing things in perspective, an approach which is definitely required when expecting a baby. After all, in the first place the child should be a goal in itself and not a way of satisfying one's own needs.

- Talk to other people, usually a bit older, who have experienced more or less the same thing. Whether they have even adopted one child or more, they may turn out to be the ideal conversation partners, now and in the future.

- Try to accept that life has limitations and that you are not the only couple who cannot have children. Notice and appreciate the good things in life. Perhaps you are enjoying perfect health, you may have a great bunch of friends, a good job, etc. In other words, once again: put life with or without children in perspective. Then the obsession you may have about the child being everything to you may disappear as well.

When, after much deliberation, you have decided to adopt a child, another problem occurs. You now have to choose a child who already exists. After all, the child you will receive is already a boy or a girl, has a certain age, is in a certain state of health and is from a certain country. Some couples will consider adopting a child from their own country first; a child that does not differ from them racially. Then, when they find out that this is extremely difficult, if not impossible, they give up. In the Netherlands, for example, people over the age of 35 are not even eligible for adopting a child born here.

Others will try to adopt a child born in another European country. But usually this is not possible either, although more children have come from Eastern European countries in the past few years. Eventually, applicant adoptive parents are left with no alternative but to adopt a child from a far-away country. I chose my formulation on purpose to make it seem that, to most parents, a racially different child is a third or fourth choice. Obviously it should not be like that. To prevent this from being the case, I will present yet more advice. Couples considering adoption had better be well-informed about the possibilities that exist. This can be learned from literature published by the adoption organisations, by conversations with other adoptive parents and from various other organisations. Then, after acquiring and processing all the necessary information, the couple are able to reach a well-thought-out decision. Then, as a couple, they can start working on a new plan. Adoption of a foreign child will involve a lot of time, effort and expense.

Parents who do not want any more children of their own
The second group of applicant adoptive parents consists of two clearly different sub-groups. The major sub-group consists of couples with two or more children

of their own. Often this group deliberately limits the number of biological children although there is a desire to raise more children in the family, or, the composition of the family is incomplete but no more biological children are wanted, for example when the family consists wholly of boys and the parents would very much like to have a girl, or the other way around. Other parents, who have a boy and a girl, deliberately want a third, or even a fourth, child to make the family more complete by giving the boy a little brother and the girl a little sister. In short, with this group, the ideas parents have about the ideal composition of the family are an influence on the motives to adopt a child.

Families with up to two children deserve our particular attention. Their number will increase relatively. Data from *Het Centraal Bureau voor de Statistiek* Central Statistics Bureau (C.B.S.), about the decrease in births until 1992, indicate that births of third children have decreased by 60 per cent. This means that two-children families determine the look of family structure more and more. It may be, however, that some of these couples desire a family expansion after several years, which may have a direct effect on the recent interest in adopting a foreign child. In the actual work of adoption organisations we come across the phenomenon of the older couple. Usually they are around forty years old with two children of their own, who are sometimes (well) over ten years old, and they want to start anew, as it were, and have young children again.

There is also the sub-group of applicant adoptive parents who have decided to adopt at a much earlier stage. Whereas the aforementioned group makes an important decision about the structure of the family fairly late, the group we are talking about here have made the adoption of one or more adoptive children part of the family-planning from the start. It is usually the fairly young aspirant adoptive parents who want an adoptive child between their own children or directly following their first or second child and then continue without conceiving any more children. In this group, other motives may play an important part (see 2.3) – as is the case with couples who choose a life without any children of their own. Until recently these have been few in number. In the 1960s the number of childless couples was estimated at 10 per cent, almost exclusively couples who remained childless involuntarily. The number of couples who do not want any children of their own has increased greatly since 1975. Te Velde (1991) states that, of Dutch women born around 1950, 15 per cent have not had any children. Over half of them are childless by choice.

2.3 Changes in motives for adoption

In 1956 the first adoption law was brought into effect in the Netherlands, and in Belgium legalisation through adoption became possible in 1969. Even without the approval of the birth parents, a Judge could authorise adoption if it was in the child's interest.

In the period preceding the early 1970s only children born in the Netherlands or Belgium and some other European countries were adopted. The majority (92%) of the people adopting were involuntarily childless. From 1972 onwards this changed. Increasingly more people with children of their own decided to adopt a child, who was nearly always from Asia, South America or Africa. Around 1980 this number rose to approximately 30 per cent. Since then it has decreased to nearly 20 per cent (Hoksbergen 1991, p.75), but the number of adoptive parents with biological children is still much larger than in the first adoption-period.

Are there reasons for these changes in our society?

Family-sociological publications show that people's ideas about having children have changed a great deal in the past decade. The decline in birth-rate is considered a symptom or consequence of these changes. Quantitively speaking, it can be said that the standard for the ideal number of children has strongly shifted downwards. What is also of importance is that nowadays, in our society, issues such as having or not having children are much more open for discussion. Ideas about parenthood are being questioned and increasingly more people seem to make conscious decisions regarding this subject. Progress in the medical field and the elaborate sex education in schools, about having children and the family, have made this technically possible and, consequently, advanced. I also think of the influence of modern media. Many adoption organisations know from experience that the choice for foreign adoption is influenced by television programmes about children and having children. Following a programme about the conditions of children in the Third World and the, merely casually mentioned, possibility of doing something about it by means of (financial) adoption, the number of applications always rises instantly. These applicants are often not the best motivated ones, for the number of people subsequently withdrawing is parallel to the number of applications.

However, the fact remains that the greater openness, the disappearance of certain taboos and the many discussions about various aspects of family life – including the option of foreign adoption – increases the interest in adoption of a foreign child. The number of people choosing adoption now is much larger than in the period when there was only the possibility of adopting children born within Europe. In those days adoption was a topic that was not easily talked about. Adoption organisations stressed the importance of the anonymity of adoptive parents. Why? Because at that time it was believed that adoptive parents would want to be left in peace after all the effort they had spent in taking a child into their family. Also, to the outside world, some adoptive parents did not want to acknowledge that they had adopted a child. In some instances people moved after they had found out that other people knew about their adoption or plans to adopt. This reservation and need for anonymity seems to have decreased. However, when parenthood is concerned with modern techniques and donors of sperm and/or ova are required, this need for anonymity rises again. Many doctors believe that secrecy about non-genetic parenthood is to be preferred, in the interest of the family and the future child. From adoption practice and research (Kirk 1981; Hoksbergen, Juffer and Waardenburg 1986), we know that the opposite is the case. Openness in parents toward the child when important family issues are concerned stimulates mutual relations. Living a lie in a family proves very difficult to keep up. A casual remark by family or friends, such as 'Peter really does(n't) take after his mum/dad!', can evoke a strange reaction in the Peter in question. Subconsciously he feels that something is not right, but he does not yet know what.

When, at a later age, Peter learns that his father is not his biological father (artificial insemination using a donor) or even that neither of his parents are his biological parents (embryo transfer using donors of sperm and ovum), this may lead to a complete break-up with his (social) parents. I have seen examples of these tragic emotional strains many times where children were involved who had a different father than they thought and only found out much later.

2.4 The choice for a particular adoptive child

While I said above that relatively more people choose adoption, at the same time only a very small part of the group of involuntarily childless couples choose adoption. It is difficult to estimate how large this group is, and it is not a fixed percentage. For Belgium, the Netherlands and the Scandinavian countries I have come to an estimate of 10 to 15 per cent. This means that people who very consciously choose children – and on top of that a very special group of children, (foreign) adoptive children – must be driven by special and powerful motives.

The explanation which Humphrey gave in 1969 about the fact that certain couples with no children do decide to adopt and others do not is interesting. When comparing two of these types of married couples (each group consisted of forty couples), he concluded that adoptive parents more often had happily married parents. The wife's relationship with her parents proved to be very important. An involuntarily childless woman who had had happy parents and who assumed that her mother had enjoyed being a parent was more inclined to adopt, in order to enjoy the same pleasant experience.

The influence of parents, friends and other acquaintances must not be under-estimated, according to some people. In 1975, an English magazine on adoption reported the experiences of a group of women in a fertility clinic. One of the women mentions that some of the worst things are questions from parents-in-law, such as 'When will we have grandchildren?' Also friends, brothers or sisters tend to casually enquire when there will (finally) be any children. Extreme feelings of guilt, and also feelings of psychological pressure to take certain steps, may come about as a result of this. In the young women's magazine *Flair*, which appears in Belgium and the Netherlands, we read 'The world outside played a very important role. I (a woman, past thirty, who is infertile) had a great need of support, understanding and sensible conversation, but women colleagues would shrug scornfully and smile "You have to go to a doctor to have a baby? All my husband has to do is wink at me from the foot of our bed and I am pregnant".'

As I said before, another group of adoptive parents has appeared, apart from the group of involuntarily childless couples. These are the people who can have as many children as they like, but, for a broad range of reasons, decide to adopt. Fear of over-population, a deeply felt concern for children in extremely hard circumstances or feelings of guilt with respect to war victims – which goes for certain American couples with regard to Korean and Vietnamese children – are motives which are frequently heard in these cases. These people want to help a 'child in need' and not just by means of financial adoption through, for example, the Foster Parents plan (in the Netherlands approximately 275,000 children are helped that way).

In a study that was finished in 1979, parents were asked to state their motives for adoption as clearly as possible. They were given a choice from one or more of this list:

1.   We were confronted with the fact that the chance of having children of our own was very small. However, we did want to start a family and thus decided to adopt our child.

2.   We clearly recognise the problem of over-population and, therefore, decided not to have any (more) children of our own. Since we did want to start a family, we decided to adopt.

3.   Amongst our friends and acquaintances we have several couples who have adopted a child. This made us very enthusiastic, so we decided to adopt a child as well.

4.   We adopted a child because children who cannot grow up with their own families have to miss out on a lot. We want to give this child that opportunity.

5.   We had contact with our child through written correspondence. When it turned out it was possible to adopt this child we decided to do just that.

6.   It is possible that you had a different motive for adopting your child. Please state your motive below.

It goes without saying that the first motive (involuntary childlessness) is marked as an answer most times. Yet half of the people questioned also explicitly indicated that the fourth motive, 'to give the child a chance', also played a part. However, most interesting is the difference between the involuntarily childless parents and parents with children of their own. Of the latter, half of the people questioned indicated that the second motive, 'danger of over-population', played a part, whereas only eight per cent of the involuntarily childless parents said so. Also, the group with children of their own mention the motive of 'to give the child a chance' somewhat more often.

Friends with adopted children proved to have influenced the decision for certain adoptive parents, and the last motive, pre-structured by us, proved to be valid for only one couple.

Looking back, it turned out that it was possible to divide motives into two groups:

- ᶜ motives with the emphasis on the family (internally oriented motives)
- ° motives with the emphasis on the adoptive child (externally oriented motives)

As far as the family directed motives are concerned, I have made a distinction between motives that have to do with the make-up of the family and motives that have more to do with the parents. The age balance of the children in the family is mentioned and the lack of a play-mate for the biological child plays a part. When the focus is on the parents, it proves again how strongly involuntary childlessness can interfere in life. With this group there are often clear medical reasons for not having any (more) children.

In the case of motives that are directed more towards the child, it is, amongst other things, a question of feelings of guilt – as demonstrated by the following remark made by an adoptive parent: 'We feel partly responsible for the consequences of the US troops who are in Vietnam for our freedom.' Apart from this fairly general concern, direct interest for the child is often mentioned, such as: 'We want to help children who have no means of existence in their own country' and 'The attention two parents can give an adoptive child and the upbringing in a family will offer the child a better chance than a children's home'.

Finally, very common human motives are mentioned, such as: 'We like children' and 'It has always been a cherished wish'. Obviously these motives play a part for almost all parents. After all, liking children and wanting to look after them is the essence of parenthood. In fact, each couple should indicate this as a motive since it is so essential. However, this probably does not even occur to most parents because it is something that goes without saying.

2.5 From internally oriented motives to externally oriented motives

When people decide to adopt a child it usually takes several years before the child is actually placed in the family. In the meantime, various changes can occur in the ideas and motives of the applicant adoptive parents. One aspect of this process of changes is sometimes jokingly called 'from white to black' by adoption organisations. Naturally this does not express the actual movement in feelings and thoughts of people. However, it does hold an element of truth. An element which I express as 'internal versus external'. This means a process involving motives for adoption in which there is, first, a question of internal orientation – towards own person and family – and, later, a strong concern for the outside world.

I distinguish three aspects to which this applies: First, we often see that involuntarily childless couples initially try, with huge effort, to have children of their own and then, after a long time, decide on adoption. This is clearly a matter of a development (out of necessity if one wants to start a family) from a biological child to an adoptive child. Then, we fairly often see that the child they have in mind initially is as near to white as possible – perhaps with the intention of making the child resemble as much as possible the biological child they never had, as far as outward appearance is concerned. Some of these people will then go through the growth process from a European adoptive child to a non-European adoptive child. Also, this aspect of the change from internal to external orientation is usually out of necessity because it is simply the case that the number of European adoptive children is much smaller than the number of non-European adoptive children. The third aspect concerns putting one's own need for a child in the family in a less central position and focusing on the 'child in need' motive.

Adoption organisations in several European countries are consciously trying to stimulate this process. The *Nederlandse Organisatie Wereldkinderen* (The Dutch Association Children of the World), for instance, is not merely an adoption organisation. In 1992 approximately two and a half million Dfl. was allocated to various projects abroad, especially Colombia, Brazil, India and the Philippines. These were funds gathered by means of various activities in the 20 regions of the association and through selling goods from the Third World. The largest aid project concerns the financial adoption of about 6000 children.

2.6 Desires with respect to the adoptive child

Preference for the country of origin

The preference of applicant adoptive parents for a certain country of origin can be related to several things. For example, where the adoption of a second child is concerned, parents usually express a strong preference for a child from the same country. To some parents, the outward appearance of the child is another important point; sometimes they have a preference for children that look the most European. However, the majority of adoptive parents do not have a preference for a specific country of origin. Obviously this is good news as it makes the procedure of 'matching' (deciding which couple is most suitable for the child in question) a lot simpler.

An interesting point is the difference between couples without children and couples with children: initially the first group more often states a preference for European countries. Again the childless couples seem more internally oriented.

Gender preference

From general experience it is known that in Western countries there is a greater preference for the adoption of girls. The well-known adoption writer, H.D. Kirk (1981), attributes this to the great store which men in particular set by a blood-line of heirs. After all, boys count as the continuation of the family; they are the so-called family heirs. Adoption of a girl would be considered less risky in this respect. However, his study is of a slightly older date and, in view of the changes in the past decade, one may assume that other explanations could be given. In addition to this, the local institutions abroad seem to detect a clear decline in this strong preference for girls. With those who do express a preference for a certain gender, there is a clear preference for girls. It is striking that couples with a child of their own prefer a girl to a boy. A partial explanation might be that quite a lot of adoptive parents think that raising girls is considerably easier than raising boys. However, in my view this is an illusion. There are, of course, clear differences between boys and girls in the problems that may occur in their upbringing and in their reactions during puberty. Boys are more strongly inclined to externalise their problems; symptoms include stronger aggressiveness, anti-social behaviour and vandalism. Girls are more inclined to bottle-up their problems and resort to depressive behaviour; they cannot be reached emotionally and are much more reticent (Verhulst and Versluis-den Bieman 1989; Geerars, 't Hart and Hoksbergen 1991)

Age preference
Whereas the number of parents who have a preference for the country of origin and the gender of the child is in fact relatively small, in both cases less than half, this is not the case for preference for the child's age. Here, by far, most parents have clear wishes. This goes for childless couples in particular. Approximately 60 per cent of them prefer a baby. It can be expected that this percentage has risen considerably, particularly as the problems of older adoptive children have received considerable publicity in the past few years. This will prevent many couples from adopting a child of, for example, three or four years old. In itself this is understandable. Involuntarily childless couples want to raise a child from as young as possible, thus experiencing all the stages of the child's development. But, naturally, the fact that a child who comes into a family at a later age brings more of a background with it also plays a part. Usually this background is a burden. Extremely horrible experiences can be reflected in the child's behaviour. It is not without reason that when a child is suitable for adoption it is recommended to have it adopted as young and as quickly as possible. However, a lot of foreign adoptive children are not helped by this. After all, many of them are a bit older when they become orphans, or abandoned by their parents and the rest of the family, at which point adoption seems the only solution. In several countries, such as India, national adoption is just getting started and the number of adoptive babies will decrease further, since these children will be adopted in their own country.

2.7 Other people's reactions to adoption plans

One aspect has hardly been talked about yet: the reactions of friends, family and others involved in the plans of an applicant adoptive couple. After all, when the matter has been well discussed among themselves, the couple will want to talk about it with other people. This can lead to influencing, for example the influence other adoptive parents may have. It has been proved that other adoptive parents often have a positive and accelerating influence on the decision-making.

This argues in favour of the supportive work done by adoption organisations. They try to supply applicant adoptive parents with as much information as possible, for instance by stimulating contacts between adoptive parents. These contacts prove to have a certain influence. Within the organisation, emphasis is put on the importance of making contact with other applicant adoptive parents who are in the same stage of the adoption procedure, even before a child is placed with the family. Experience and feelings can then be exchanged and one has the opportunity to contemplate the step that has been taken and the preferences that have been expressed. Once the decision to adopt has been made, grandparents, family, friends and neighbours often react positively. The reactions from grand-parents deserve some attention, because there are clear differences. First, we see that both grandparents on the mother's side react more positively than the grandparents on the father's side. The fact that the reaction is, on average, less positive from the grandparents on the father's side is not solely a European phenomenon. In their study of 34 American couples, Grow and Shapiro (1975) mention the same difference in reactions by grandparents of adoptive children.

This may have to do with the difference in the way in which parents of grown-up children play a part in the lives of their children. Apparently, the wife's parents are more important than the husband's where certain family matters are concerned. It probably also has to do with the role differences between the husband and the wife. After all, it is a fact that women are more strongly involved with the emotional aspects of family life. Also, we often see that women are the ones taking the initiative where adoption plans are concerned. It is, therefore, fairly self-evident that she will consult her own parents before consulting her husband's parents, for they may be confronted more intensively with the needs and desires of the adoptive mother-to-be. Finally, it may very well be true that women show their feelings more clearly and openly than men. In other words, it fits our culture image to think that the grandparents on the mother's side, in particular the grandmother, are generally more involved. Perhaps the grandparents on the father's side have a greater interest in the blood-line and regard an adoptive child as 'second best'.

Although most of the reactions of other people were predominantly positive, the differences are interesting enough to make another distinction between the group of childless couples and the couples with children. The idea existed that reactions by a third party to the adoption plans of childless couples would be slightly more positive than reactions to adoption plans from people with natural children. Many family members and friends, especially those directly involved, would be able to understand very well how important such a step was for a childless couple. This 'understanding' would be expressed in the way they reacted. It has been proved from research that the reactions to plans made by childless couples are more often distinctly positive than reactions to adoption plans of couples with children. In addition to this, grandparents on the father's side react least positively, especially when it concerns couples with children. All these matters are probably related to the difference in motivation between both groups of adoptive parents. Perhaps this conscious planning of a family, and the fact that foreign adoption is considered a useful alternative, does not appeal to an older generation. Unfamiliarity with the phenomenon of adoption and prejudices probably also play a part in this. Because of this one may feel less involved with the children's family-planning.

I dare not make any predictions as to what extent these views have changed or perhaps will change. As it happens, conflicting developments are taking place. On the one hand there is greater openness between people and a decrease of the taboo subjects, such as sexuality, infertility and adoption, as a lot more is known about the needs of children in many countries and, because of this, it will be easier for parents with plans to adopt to communicate. On the other hand, population density has risen a great deal in countries such as the Netherlands and Belgium. We have to bear in mind that the number of people requesting political refuge has increased sharply, and also we are faced with family formations of foreigners. This development may lead to a more critical approach towards foreign adoption.

CHAPTER 3

Adoptive Parents Need Intensive Preparation

3.1 Even when everything seems ready, things can still go wrong

For adoptive parents, 'expecting a baby' takes a very peculiar form. Most couples have to spend ten to twenty hours on a plane and, more often than not, have to arrange the final papers in a far-away country. Others have to wait at the arrivals terminal at an airport somewhere in Europe, Australia, New Zealand or the US until the silver stork delivers the long-expected baby into their arms. Only when the parents set foot on home soil, together with their child, or when the attendant (escort, according to flight jargon) hands the parents their child, are the adoptive parents certain that nothing can go wrong procedure-wise. However, it is fortunate that when a certain child is allocated to a couple abroad – which usually happens by means of a court judgement – the chance of the child's arrival is very great.

Still, things can go wrong at the very last minute. Most tragic is when the child passes away during the procedure time. Fortunately this happens rarely but this risk really does exist, especially with very young children of, for example, a few days or a few weeks old. Children may also be claimed at the very last moment by either the birth parents or relatives. This does happen where the children are responsible for the continuation of the family name, as is the case with boys or eldest girls. This too happens only occasionally. These last-minute withdrawals do, however, illustrate the difficulty of giving up a child, even in a broader family context.

It has also happened that a country temporarily (Sri Lanka, China), or permanently (Bangladesh, Indonesia), closes its borders to children who leave the country for adoption abroad.

Less definite, but nonetheless taxing for adoptive parents, and the child too as it gets older, are the – relatively frequent – delays during the course of the adoption procedure. This can happen, for instance, when a judge suddenly requires supplementary information as certain details appear to be missing or when there are certain changes in the procedure. Courts of law are at times non-active. A court of law may have a new judge, who requires the necessary administrative changes. The child may get ill, seriously or not, and it would be irresponsible to let him go with such a long flight ahead. Strikes abroad which, for instance, impede the functioning of the courts or air traffic have also caused unnecessary excitement and tension.

In short, only when the child sets foot on home soil are the adoptive parents able to relax. Although even then serious risks still exist. For instance, it has happened several times that a child died shortly after his arrival.

3.2 Useful preparations for the adoptive parents when the child is due

Preparations on the social level

Finally the long period of waiting is over. All the signs indicate that the child will finally arrive. Naturally the parents need to make the necessary preparations. This may be purely practical, such as adapting the living conditions, preparing a room in the house for the arrival of the newcomer, buying children's clothes, toys and such like. When adoptive parents get an older child it is sensible to visit people who have a child of the same age, to get an idea of what is needed. At the same time, it is useful to get some information as to what a child of that age can and does do. Any potential delay in development will then be spotted quickly. However, one must bear in mind that the child must first adapt itself to a completely new situation. So do not pass judgement or be disappointed too quickly about the child's abilities. In the next chapter I will deal with this more extensively.

The preparations can also be on a more communicative level. Other relatives, especially any biological children within the family, will have to be told that the family expansion which has sometimes been discussed will now in fact occur. One might perhaps want to contact other adoptive parents to experience support yet again or, at the very least, hear how they experienced it at the time. With regard to the latter, research has again shown how fellow-adoptive parents play an important part in the entire process. Almost 90 per cent of adoptive parents had contact with other adoptive parents before the arrival of their child, and half of these couples reported these contacts as 'very valuable'. Only a small minority felt these contacts had been of little importance and did not serve as support. If parents collect the child together with other couples, these contacts will often continue to exist for years. Thus children from the same orphanage also get the chance to maintain these contacts to some extent.

If there are one or more children in the family already the parents will have to tell them that a new child will join the family. The best moment to do this obviously depends on the age of the children in the family. Children younger than approximately six years have little notion of time. To announce the arrival of the new-comer six months in advance is not very useful. For a few days it will lead to all sorts of questions and, subsequently, to great misunderstanding and confusion in the child. It might be helpful to hang a calendar in the house and together mark off days gone by. The child can then keep it up by himself and see how much longer it will be. The extent to which the children are left insecure is of importance because children nearly always respond positively to the news and it is of great importance to consider when the time is right to tell them. It should, certainly, not be too early.

With older children the subject of adoption can, and should, be discussed more thoroughly. They need to be intensively involved and their opinions sought. This needs to occur at an early stage, when the idea first occurs to the parents. Even though the initial response may not be positive in some cases, the children can then at least get accustomed to the idea. When the response of children of approximately eight years and older is negative, serious attention needs to be paid. There are aspirant adoptive parents who have abandoned their plans due to the response of their children. Many children will experience the arrival of a new child as something surprising and exciting: for children who are an only child, it does, in fact, mean a new playmate.

What is most important is to make it clear to the children from the start that there are plans but it is not at all certain that they will go through. However, when the parents have every reason to believe that the children would dearly like another brother or sister, it is probably better to wait until the arrival is almost certain and tangible details are known about the adoptive child.

Preparing the children for the arrival of the adoptive child should, in any case, not just be an announcement. The children should be guided and encouraged to look forward to the new situation together with the parents.

Practical preparations

The arrival of a child requires all sorts of immediate preparations. A room has to be prepared for the child. In this aspect, the only difference with a natural birth is that the newcomer is 'somewhat' older. However, in the field of employment benefits there are differences. Many companies and government institutions provide for maternity leave. However, there is, as yet, no law on maternity leave. Should a similar provision not be necessary when we think of people who want to (or have to) fetch their child from abroad themselves? One may argue about the amount of time which is to be compensated. One must bear in mind that many adoptive parents have to stay in Asia or South America for weeks. After the arrival of the child, both parents need to thoroughly adjust themselves to the new situation. The question remains whether, if the adoptive mother has a job, paid leave should also be eight weeks. After all, maternity leave is based on the idea that the mother should get the opportunity to feed the child herself and recover from childbirth.

We presented various preliminary preparations in the following question: 'We have gathered several preparations which adoptive parents might have made for the arrival of their son/daughter into the family. Could you indicate which preparations (one or more) you have made?'

Both adoptive parents do have the need to completely focus on the child for some time. A good half of the fathers took a week or more off work and a further 15 per cent one or a few days. Nearly the same applies to working mothers.

So many fathers consciously taking time off work is a result of advice by the social workers and other people of the adoption organisation involved. Experience has taught us that the arrival of an adoptive child means a large emotional burden for both parents, but particularly for the mother. Subsequently, it is very important that, especially in the difficult initial phase, the parents are supportive of one another and are thus able to create a good starting climate for the child. For some countries an adoptive mother with a job outside the home is reason enough to question the motives for adopting a child more deeply. Sometimes there are obvious doubts and the adoptive mother needs to be prepared to (temporarily) stop working if the raising of the child appears to demand this.

In direct relation to this, almost half of the adoptive parents questioned by us asked relatives and friends not to come by at first. We would like to emphasise the necessity of this. Parents and child quietly need the time to get used to one another. Think of all the changes for the child! There was the departure from the children's home or from the biological parents; there were strange escorts on the flight to whom, in all the upheaval, the child clung; the long flight itself. Because of the many different people who looked after the child in such a short time, the child may (temporarily) lose all idea as to whom he belongs – especially when he is at an age (up to approximately four years old) where he cannot yet understand what is going to happen. In addition to this, there is the fact that, due to many changes in the country of origin, the children often lack any basic security. The parents who fetch the child themselves have met him in his old environment and accompany him on the plane themselves. Especially when the adoption of older children is concerned (from two years onwards), it is better for parents to fetch the child themselves. However, the possible disadvantage of accompaniment by strange escorts must not be overestimated. After all, they have a great deal of experience with children in this situation and, at the same time, know that emotional ties with the child should be avoided as much as possible during the flight.

A small percentage of the parents had to move in view of the arrival of the child. Most of these because the present housing was too small. However, some couples said that the social surroundings exercised such pressure that they thought it better to leave and start afresh somewhere else. The latter also occurs with the arrival of biological children. A family can feel very uncomfortable in a certain neighbourhood, but not find this as important for themselves. However, as soon as children arrive, they do decide to move.

Finally, some couples appear to have moved somewhere else temporarily – an arrangement which, in view of the arrival of the child, is not to be recommended. At that moment the priority needs to be to get the child quietly accustomed to her new surroundings. Therefore it is best to stay at home as much as possible in the beginning. However, when one does have to go out, or visit others, it is best to take the child along. The child needs to get the feeling as soon as possible that people and situations are permanent.

Considering all the above, it should be clear that the preparations for the arrival of the adoptive child differ greatly depending on its age. Every preparation for an adoptive child needs to be intensive and well thought out. But, especially with a child of about 12 months or older, parents would do well to go to others for advice and both take plenty of time for adjustment after the arrival. I strongly discourage dropping the child off everyday or having it looked after by different people at home whilst both parents go to work. There is a great risk that the child will adjust far more slowly because feelings of security, safety and trust in people are given less chance.

CHAPTER 4

The Arrival of the Child
Changes the Family

4.1 What should parents pay attention to?

For parents who fetch their child themselves, the first period of familiarisation and adaptation to the child begins in a foreign country, often under mentally aggravating and tiring circumstances. Perhaps many will experience the homecoming as the true beginning of adaptation. In any case, for the child it is then that the big transition takes place. Naturally, the information which was given to the child about what is going to happen has a great influence on the child. What image has the child formed about the future with those strange people in that far-away country who will be his parents?

Adoptive parents would do well to thoroughly find out roughly what can be expected of a child of a certain age. This will have to be done anyway because of various practical matters such as buying clothes, toys and the like. Talking to people with children in the same age group is definitely to be recommended. Again I point out the importance of maintaining contact with other (adoptive) parents, especially where the adoption of an older child is concerned, as the first period will be full of pitfalls.

Language problems, which can be extremely annoying, take up a large part. Having a simple list with highly frequent words (father, mother, eating, drinking, sleeping, etc.) is very useful. Obviously, it makes quite a difference which country the child is from and which language she is familiar with. Most likely it will be easier for European parents to overcome the language barrier with a child from a Spanish speaking country (such as Colombia), than with a child from an Asian country A beginner's course in Spanish, Portuguese etc. is recommended, particularly for parents who are picking up the child themselves. These things tend to run a little smoother when there are other children in the family already. It is striking how easily children 'understand' each other. Other children can sometimes function as intermediaries between the parents and the adoptive child.

27

Although language problems can be difficult at first, we have learnt from experience that they seem to pass fairly quickly. Time and time again it is miraculous to see how quickly a young child understands things, or at least, *seems* to understand them. Like other young growing children, the adoptive child quickly acquires a passive command of the foreign language. She understands various matters, but cannot yet express in words what goes on in her mind. It usually takes a little longer for the child to start speaking Dutch, Flemish or French, which again is dependent on the age of the child. Parallel to this we see the native language disappear rapidly, sometimes with the exception of a few very specific words. However, I should express a few words of warning here. First, children older than approximately 2 years will often start using a type of transitional language, a type of broken Flemish/Dutch (de Vries 1987). This can go on for several years. The language problems often concern word order, use of articles, word gender, using the correct preposition and the conjugation of verbs. When the children have grown older they will, in relation to the direct language problems, be inclined to pretend they understand what is said or asked. This is why I said 'seems to understand' above. Because many adoptive children cope with extremely difficult situations ('survival of the fittest' applies to most of them!), they can react in an independent and self-assured manner in certain practical situations. Moreover, the child will want to understand everything to satisfy the adults. Thus, language-ignorance is compensated for by means of 'knacks' and carefully taking notice of what the child thinks has to be done. Consequently the parents may think that the child does understand these things. However, particularly complicated (abstract) expressions or phrases should be explained extensively and it should be checked whether the child understands them at all. A Swedish researcher, Gardell (1980), found that children between 18 months and 3 years old when they arrive are most vulnerable with regard to language-adaptation. According to Gardell, this is because the separation from parents and country of origin is much more drastic at that particular stage of development. During the first years of life, a child forms a picture of the world in a concrete manner, using all his senso-motoric capacities (looking, listening, seizing, moving, recalling). Ordinarily, between 18 months and 3 years, the development of a child reaches a level at which it becomes possible to start thinking with the use of slightly symbolic internal images. These symbols are founded on a passive knowledge of words which the child acquires through contact with other people, mainly his caretakers. The child himself has reached a phase in which he actively starts to use one-word sentences and more-word sentences. With emigration to another country, an abrupt stop occurs in this development. In the case of these children, this may be called a language-shock. Also, the self-awareness which takes shape from the first year onwards can become severely impaired. When everything which is familiar is lost, the child seems to be left to himself and his stubborn attitude (especially between 1 and 2 years old), which make the child even more insecure than he already was because of all the changes. To children of this age it is especially difficult to explain just what is about to happen.

An additional factor which is a strong influence in the first period after placement in the family concerns the habits which the child had acquired in the meantime: a certain way to dress, how to eat, sleep, how to behave around adults and the like. Especially in the first period, the extent to which a child is attached to certain habits or things will partly determine the child's behaviour, particularly when the adoptive parents do not, or cannot, realise this. Therefore one has to be on the alert when the child reacts in a violently rejecting manner in certain situations. The reasons for this kind of behaviour can be identified fairly easily, for example refusing help with going to the toilet, seeing a particular kind of food – which is quite familiar to us – for the first time, or not knowing certain habits – such as being taken to bed by the father. Obviously an ideal situation would be when the adoptive parents know so much about the child, his background and habits that they can anticipate things which are perfectly normal for the child.

As far as the attachment to certain things is concerned, it is of the greatest importance to treat these things with gentle care and always save all the things that the child has brought with him. Give the child the opportunity to show what he has grown attached to. This may be a silly little toy or piece of clothing which does not seem very attractive to us. Children can attach themselves very strongly to certain specific things, especially when they were given to them by a person dear to them. Also, later on, when the child becomes more curious of his background, these objects may be of great emotional importance. When the child sees that the parents have saved everything, he will realise that they thought it important, which will come across as a positive gesture. With respect to this, I always advise parents to make a book about the history of the child's life. A book in which the history of the child, from the first contact with the adoptive parents, is recorded by means of pictures, clippings, notes of peculiar utterances of the child, important happenings and happy moments. Especially for adoptive children, and the future adolescent/adult, information about their life history is very important. He or she already has to do without a large part of his/her history. Having a lot of precise information from the start of his/her life with the adoptive parents is at least something.

An important question for adoptive parents is, of course, whether the child will grow attached to them – preferably as strongly as if the child were their own. In 1993, Femmie Juffer finished a study for the Adoption Centre in co-operation with the University of Leiden. She studied whether adoptive children from Sri Lanka and South Korea were able to grow attached to their new parents and whether this could be stimulated. It concerned 90 children, all less than six months old when they arrived.

The results of her study are hopeful. She concludes 'that in adoptive families as often as in biological families there is a safe attachment in the first childhood years' (Juffer 1993, p.222). She has also developed a programme for instruction on upbringing for adoptive parents. For this she compiled a booklet called 'The first year of life' and used video recordings of several contact scenes between mother and child. The use of video recordings, and the discussion about them, worked well in stimulating reactions of the mother to the child and the attachment of the child to the mother.

Obviously, it is important to realise that Juffer's study deals with children who arrive as a baby. Will the parent–child attachment run equally well with children who are twelve months or older on arrival? Would it be possible to stimulate those as well? These are questions which the Adoption Centre will try to answer by means of research started in 1994.

4.2 Specific medical details of the child

Time and time again, the overall physical condition or health of the child proves to be a great influence on the child's behaviour. Because of a poor state of health or a specific disorder, a child can be impeded in activities that are normal for other children of that age. Sometimes there is the risk that so much attention has to be paid to the medical treatment of the child that little time is left for the actual upbringing and changes in habits and behaviour. There is also the risk of denying the other children in the family the necessary attention.

Before a child comes to Europe a medical statement has to be made, in which any serious diseases the child may have are mentioned. Usually information about the more general physical condition of the child is also given. The quality of these statements of health given by the countries of origin often leave much to be desired, according to our standards. This is due, in part, to the fact that the diagnostic facilities in these countries cannot be compared with those in Europe. When a child who comes from a far-away children's home which hardly has any money to feed the children, let alone provide proper medical facilities, is visited by a local doctor, the risks of incomplete information about the physical condition are enormous – no matter how good the intentions of the doctor in question.

The specification of the age of the child is a different matter altogether. It happens fairly often that, with hindsight, the age of the child does not tally. For this there can be several reasons: Where an abandoned child is concerned, an estimate has to be made about the age. Where it concerns a severely neglected child, there may be impaired growth and development. In such cases the child's age is very easily under-estimated. It happens that, for instance, a three-year-old child cannot walk properly yet. Another reason has to do with the pragmatism of the institution. After all, as the child is younger it becomes easier to have him adopted. So, very practical reasons can play a part in the 'mistakes' concerning the age of the child.

With certain children there is a known age difference of two or more years. A child who was supposedly five years old turned out to be eight years old after radiographic examination. With such a large age difference, problems may arise in school later – such as not feeling at home with children of that age group and a seemingly premature puberty. Problems may arise initially at home, too, and in some families the problems turn out to be serious enough to necessitate transference fairly soon. In any case, it is important to always have an age check done when abandoned children are involved. This is relatively simple and not at all disturbing for the child.

Do adoptive parents have an unacceptably greater chance of having a child with medical peculiarities that they were not expecting? This is only partly the case. According to American paediatricians, seven or eight per cent of all American babies have some minor, or more serious, defects at birth. The majority of these defects are easy to recognise and within a period of six months after birth practically all medical defects will have been identified. There are three exceptions to this:

1. certain defects of internal organs, such as the urinary system; or biochemical disorders, such as diabetes.

2. degenerative diseases, such as muscular dystrophy, which only become visible at a later stage.

3. certain brain disorders.

However, the chances of these defects are rather small. The fact that many adoptive children arrive at a later age makes the risk of not discovering any defects smaller. But certain risks remain. In this respect, adoptive parents are no better off than biological parents. A study conducted in 1980 concerning adoptive parents with disabled children showed a whole range of medical problems, including harelip, polio, loss of a limb, slight brain damage, spina bifida, clubfoot and tuberculosis.

Therefore, all adoptive parents must pay a visit to the family doctor immediately after the child has arrived, with a medical checklist, which in several European countries are customarily provided by the adoption organisations. The child can then undergo a specific screening. Furthermore, adoptive parents should not hesitate to ask for referral to a specialist at an early stage. After all, we should realise that many European doctors know little about tropical diseases or the consequences of, for instance, malnutrition because these diseases hardly ever occur here.

From several scientific studies which have been conducted since 1970, we know what kind of medical problems adoptive parents have to reckon with. Most frequent is a varying degree of malnutrition, concerning at least 30 to 40 per cent of the children. Malnutrition has various symptoms – such as hunger oedema, which often manifests itself in an accumulation of fluids in the stomach, serious weight loss, muscle-fatigue and general weakness. Apart from malnutrition, many parents mention intestinal and abdominal disorders. Often added to this is a serious parasitic infection (e.g. roundworm or tapeworm). Persistent diarrhoea is often the consequence of abdominal disorders. Parents would do well to check the faeces for a while and to insist on a precise and intensive examination when the child suffers from prolonged diarrhoea. On the whole, diarrhoea frequently occurs in adoptive children. Another complaint concerns various forms of skin diseases (scabies, eczema, fungal infections and abscesses). Scabies, which is highly infectious, is mentioned quite a few times. Partly in connection with skin diseases, parents often mention the presence of all sorts of parasites (lice). The number of children who arrive with a skin problem is countless, as experience has taught us. The change in diet, which is especially considerable for, for instance, Asian children, can cause new problems. All the more reason to be careful and on the alert with respect to changes in stools.

Of the 2236 foreign adoptive children who arrived in the Netherlands in 1984 and 1985, the paediatrician N. Sorgedrager medically examined 1003 (Sorgedrager 1988). The results of this extensive and carefully conducted study highly correspond with the results of the study conducted in 1979 and after. The data from this medical study are very important to applicant adoptive parents, which is why I will go into it extensively here.

The four main countries of origin were: Sri Lanka (41%), Korea (17.5%), Colombia (16%) and India (15%). Seventy-two per cent of the children were 12 months old or younger. Sorgedrager found that the information from the countries of origin was very scanty. As we will already know from previously mentioned research, many children (32%) suffered from some type of skin disease. Highly infectious scabies was the most frequent. Apart from this, many parents (15%) turned out to have used the services of an Ear, Nose and Throat specialist. Other parts of the body – eyes, ears, heart, lungs, stomach (often swollen liver in connection with malnutrition) and external genital problems with boys – also required medical treatment. Sorgedrager also used laboratory analysis. Anaemia (lack of iron), various liver disorders, parasitic infections and bacilli (salmonella) occurred rather frequently.

During the first two years after arrival, height and weight were studied. As many as seven per cent of the children weighed less than 2500 grammes when they arrived. In all, nearly one third of the children arrived seriously underweight. With respect to height, 22 per cent of the boys and 31 per cent of the girls showed a distinct lack of growth. As the children gained considerable height and weight after arrival, we can conclude that there were definite deficiencies in growth – even after allowing for racial differences. Because it can take several years for a child to gain substantial increases in height and weight we do not yet know if these children fully catch up.

I can illustrate this by means of two actual examples: A child aged three months weighed only 2000 grammes on arrival and a twenty-month-old child weighed no more than 6.7 kilos and was only 68 centimetres tall (80 to 90 centimetres would be normal).

Some children arrived with a runny nose – to the utter amazement of some parents who think that this occurs to a lesser extent, or not at all, in warm countries.

Apart from the ordinary cold in the nose, some children suffered from bronchitis. Various ear defects are mentioned as well. A lack of resistance as a result of malnutrition and an overall poor condition are a fertile breeding ground for all sorts of infections. When, on top of this, the diseases have been completely neglected, the consequences can be serious and long-term. In the study finished in 1979, some parents mentioned perforated eardrums and a serious degree of deafness as 'ear defects'. The deafness can lead to speech disorders, which was also mentioned (in some cases). Eye defects occurred rather frequently, sometimes due to contagious infections, but also squints and partial sightlessness. So, parents should be warned. Since older adoptive children are very good at compensating for any defects, at school as well as at home, certain sensory defects will not be easily recognised. Therefore, a thorough medical check-up is always required.

Looking over this entire gamut of medical details, one may conclude that it is quite a lot. But it is also clear that most of these defects can be cured. As Sorgedrager states: 'Some exceptional syndromes apart, only easily treatable diseases are diagnosed in adoptive children from Third World countries upon their arrival in the Netherlands' (1988).

However, sound medical care (including dentistry) and parental care remain a prerequisite. But, and I repeat this once again, the other children in the family should not be neglected in the difficult first phase after the arrival of the adoptive child. In connection with this, it should be pointed out that, from a medical point of view, some diseases and infections can be rather contagious. This can have extremely unpleasant consequences. Negligent treatment of, for example, head lice and scabies – which are often found in adoptive children – can very easily lead to infection of the other members of the family. Naturally this should be prevented as much as possible – particularly where there are older children in the family. If they 'inherit' something from the adoptive child, this may lead to extremely negative reactions towards the newcomer in the family.

Many parents may wonder about the permanency of certain disorders, especially when a child arrives with signs of serious malnutrition and additional symptoms such as extensive physical and mental deficiencies, despite the fact that, with most children, the medical problems prove to be less than expected. It is perfectly understandable that parents are afraid that this will have permanent consequences for the child. From our research we may conclude that the children have a remarkable ability for recovery. Few children take longer than several years to get over their medical problems.

4.3 The consequences of malnutrition

Research has been conducted into the consequences of malnutrition in the United States. I consider the results of this research to be so important that I want to deal with it more elaborately. After all, malnutrition is a characteristic of adoptive children that a lot of adoptive parents come across. Winick, Meyer and Harris

(1976) set out to discover the consequences of malnutrition for children who were adopted in America before attaining three years of age, suddenly found themselves in much improved conditions. They studied three groups of children. Only Korean girls were chosen, because differences in development between the sexes had to be avoided. The age on arrival in the USA was on average 18 months and no more than 3 years old. Each group consisted of approximately 50 children, differing in height and weight according to Korean standards. There was a group with undernourished children (1), fairly well fed children (2) and well fed children (3). At the time of the research all the children were to be attending primary school, as the researchers also required information about the progress the children made at school. By means of a questionnaire, the parents were asked for information about the state of health, height and weight of the child and some socio-economic information. Information about intelligence tests the children had been subjected to previously, and their achievements at school, was collected through the schools. On average, the children had been in the USA for 7 years.

The results of this study are summarised below:

- On average, the girls in all three groups were heavier and taller than could be expected according to Korean standards. However, according to American standards they remained slightly below average, which the researchers thought could be attributed to racial differences.

- For all four characteristics that were examined (height, weight, intelligence and achievements at school), there were differences between group 1 (undernourished), group 2 (fairly well fed) and group 3 (well fed). The group with underfed girls scored the least points, followed by group 2 and subsequently group 3.

- In the intelligence tests, and with the achievements at school, group 1 scored as many points as average American children. The other two groups averaged slightly better.

From the results of this study of a group of undernourished children who, however, were adopted at a young age, it appears that a near-complete recovery is very well possible – providing that, after the period of malnutrition, the children end up in a better situation for a prolonged length of time.

Now, can we think of an explanation for this? I think I may infer that adoptive parents, as a group, form a positive selection. This is hardly surprising in view of the aforementioned strong motivation for parenthood and the selection process. This is why it can be explained that children in group 2 and 3 do better than an average group of American children. After all, it is true that, by and large, parents pay more attention to their adoptive child; the entire parental care is more intensive, more conscious and more stimulating.

Why did I write above that undernourished children have made a 'near' complete recovery? Because, if the period of malnutrition did not have a permanent effect, the achievements should have been better for all three groups, especially in view of the parental care. However, this is not the case. In order to achieve average results, though only measured in terms of IQ and achievements at school, the group of underfed children need a parental environment which strongly stimulates them.

4.4 Behavioural peculiarities

How will the child behave in the future and how will he fit into our family? These are the principal questions and worries of every adoptive couple. They hope and expect the child to truly feel at home after the first (difficult) preparatory period. They hope that it will hardly be noticeable that the child was not born to them.

Many parents accept it as being obvious that children, who are actually being placed into a different culture and subsequently approached in a completely different manner, will exhibit various problems of adaptation. They also know that these problems will last for a certain period of time, depending on the age on arrival and the history in the country of origin.

First, we will pay attention to the nature and treatment of certain specific behavioural problems the children may have during their first few months in the family. As before, we will do this with respect to physical aspects.

Sleep

During children's development, various types of behaviour can occur which are nothing special at a certain age but which are a cause for concern at a later age (such as bedwetting and thumb sucking). When these occur they should be of a temporary nature. The upbringing is focused on making these types of behaviour disappear. If this is unsuccessful, the behaviour can be the result of deeper feelings of discomfort, fear, insecurity, displeasure, etc. These causes should be investigated first. The behaviour in question should then be regarded as a symptom of a deeper cause. Due to the, at times, extremely difficult circumstances and sad experiences of our adoptive children, various fending- and venting-off mechanisms may have been developed, which strike us as specific types of behaviour.

Most frequent are the problems concerning sleeping behaviour. An obvious explanation is that, especially in the first few days, the child undergoes a lot of stress. The long flight and the many new people and impressions are hardly beneficial to the child's rest. However, there is a second, more important, cause for sleeping problems. Our sleeping habits (a room of our own, usually in a separate room) may differ strongly from what the child is used to. Various examples are known of the problems this may lead to. For example, a one-year-old Vietnamese child explained that she used to have a barred bed and now, accidentally, ended up in a closed one. When the parents had made the necessary changes, the sleeping problems were solved immediately. In another case concerning a seven-year-old Colombian boy it was necessary that he went to sleep in a big cardboard box for a while, because he was used to doing that in Colombia. For eight months the parents in question tried their best to understand, and to prevent the boy from walking around restlessly at night after he had first slept for one hour. The box turned out to be the solution to the problem and the sleeping problems disappeared instantly. After having slept in his box for about two months, the boy switched to his bed again nearly all by himself. All the parents had done was give a careful suggestion that it is warmer to sleep in a normal bed during the winter.

It also happens (sometimes) that children only get sleeping problems several weeks or months later. This especially occurs in older children. In this case there are two possible causes:

First of all it may be a delayed reaction. Immediately upon arrival the child is too exhausted and unable to stay awake. But, as the child becomes more relaxed he is able to ponder and try to cope with everything that has happened. Certain changes, such as the great amount of attention and love which, all of a sudden, are given to him by the new parents and, perhaps, other people are very stressful. Fears may arise about all this being only temporary, that something bad will happen again – especially with children who have experienced sudden changes before. Many of our adoptive children have experienced one or more of those changes. For example, a mother or father dies or has suddenly disappeared, or a beloved caregiver in a children's home is replaced by someone else, or similar changes which are often disastrous for these children.

A second cause may be a subtle change in the parents' behaviour, at least in the experience of the child. In the first few weeks the child has tried his very best to show his best possible side; he exhibits what is sometimes called 'hotel behaviour' or pseudo-adaptation. Perhaps he was spoiled more in the beginning, on the one hand as a reaction to the exemplary behaviour and on the other hand as an expression of emotions which the parents have bottled up for a long time. It is not without reason that these children are called 'the most wanted children in the world'. Neither one nor the other can be kept up. Gradually the child will provoke the first negative reactions. Little by little he will acquire a slightly more normal behavioural pattern. Because of this, tension and conflicts may arise, with which the child can only cope with great difficulty. Consequently he goes to bed worried and not relaxed, which leads to sleeping problems, restlessness, bad dreams and suchlike.

The so-called 'negative' behaviour of the child can also be a conscious testing of the parents and exploring the boundaries as to what is acceptable and what is not. All children have such periods of trying out and exploring their boundaries. Since for an adoptive child the change is always great, some children will have to try out certain things again, not only materially, but also socially. Sometimes this testing starts soon after arrival, but not always. There is a positive side to this testing and boundary seeking behaviour too. I call this the second adoption paradox. Because the child abandons the hotel behaviour and starts behaving in a more normal manner and, therefore, also more negatively, the process of feeling at home with these particular parents has finally really started. So, the negative behaviour is a sign of something quite positive and important.

Finally, some practical advice in order to diminish sleeping problems. Having to sleep alone while being used to noise, the coming and going and the commotion and comfort of a dormitory tends to lead to problems. When the family consists of more children the solution is at hand. Let the child sleep with one of the other children in one room. When the child is a first-born, it may be necessary for the parents to go to bed together with the child. Giving the child a radio to take to bed might also help. The point is to make the child feel that she is not alone, or that she has not been left alone. Such measures should always be used for a fairly long period of time, usually a few weeks or months.

Eating problems

Nearly 30 per cent of the children appear to have an uncontrollable need for food. They keep on eating and as long as there is still food left on the table they will continue to fill their plates. It is possible that actual medical problems are the reason for the enormous need for food. After all, in the last section I mentioned that many children suffer from various kinds of bowel disorders. On the one hand there may be parasites which 'share in the food' while on the other hand it may be that the body absorbs the food insufficiently, which increases the need for food in order to achieve satisfaction.

One must also realise that, especially during the first year after arrival, some children are catching up on lost ground. At times this leads to exceptionally fast growth which, naturally, requires extra proteins and carbohydrates.

But it is not only medical causes that play a part. Previously most of the adoptive children were in a situation where they had to fight to survive. They know that a shortage of food means hunger and, because of this, they have learnt that what little food there is should be eaten to at least stay alive. For a long time our extravagance in throwing away excess food, is something that is so incomprehensible that it cannot and should not happen. In addition to this, they have never had the security of knowing that there will be food again the next day, so it is of vital importance to always save what is left over. This is why, in the beginning, one should not confront the (older) child with large meals where a lot is likely to be left over. Let him slowly grow accustomed to our abundance and measure the amounts of food. Do not throw away any food in the child's presence. Do not give any food that was meant for humans to pet animals. An example of the latter: not realising the consequences of her child's experiences, an adoptive mother almost caught a cold when feeding the ducks. The little four-year-old boy almost jumped into the water after the pieces of bread because he was so upset about it being thrown away.

Children – as well as adults, for that matter – sometimes start eating excessively when they do not feel at ease, or when they are nervous or feel they are not getting enough attention. It is as if the immense need for attention seeks (oral) satisfaction. Sometimes the mother in question reacts in a well-intentioned way and is inclined to stuff the child. Particularly when feeding babies, mothers tend to pay little attention to the precise amounts and need to be warned explicitly. This is probably partly a reaction from the parents to the undernourished child. They are glad that he does eat and hope that he will soon be up to scratch. For that matter, most parents are worried about whether their child eats sufficiently.

However, the opposite, eating too little or not at all, also occurs, be it less often. Usually this is due to medical factors, although the refusal of food by children can also indicate an attitude of protest. Obviously, one should seek assistance when this situation is apparent.

Relational problems

At first, contact with the new parents and any other children and people in the neighbourhood often causes problems. We may see exceptionally nice, affectionate and well-adjusted behaviour – often to everyone, even strangers – in the hope of gaining positive attention, or we may see a very expectant, or even fending-off, type of behaviour which often makes the parents feel that the child is beyond reach. To parents, the latter is very difficult to deal with. After all, it does not fit in with the expectations about how things will be once the newcomer has come to the family. These relationship problems are not always merely temporary adaptation problems. Sometimes, parents with children who arrived at an older age conclude that, in the relationship with the child, several initial problems will always remain. I should, however, say some more here about the connection between the age on arrival and various relational and social problems. Various studies (Hoksbergen, Juffer and Waardenburg 1986; Verhulst and Versluis-den Bieman 1989) have established that this relationship is not as unambiguous as might be expected. It is not the case that since the child is older on arrival it can be expected that more problems will arise. Children who arrive at a very early age can exhibit serious behavioural problems straight away and later on during puberty. From the research that was conducted among 116 children from Thailand it appeared that:

- ° Even in the group with the youngest children, 25 per cent exhibit adaptation problems

- ° The greatest difference exists between the group of children who are 6 months or younger on arrival and those who arrive at an age of 7 to 12 months

- ° It is the problematic background rather than the actual age on arrival that is the principal cause for adaptation problems.

This last point is of the greatest importance. When this happens repeatedly, I advise parents to locate as much information about their child as possible. If they pick up the child themselves, this can be done more easily. Talking with caregivers in the children's home or with others who have looked after the child, asking questions about the child's experiences in the home or possible former families, copying various documents and the like can yield more information than seemed available initially.

Another important thing appeared from the Thai research. In 19 out of the 116 children the initial problems remained in some form, and were still fairly noticeable about eight years later when we approached them for the first study.[1] So, temporary problems can be the breeding ground for permanent relational problems within the family and parents should not misjudge the allegedly temporary nature of these types of behavioural problems. Once again it is best to alert other adoptive parents or a therapist as soon as possible. For me, this conclusion is another reason to strongly advise parents to make use of after-care facilities as provided by the child welfare organisation or the adoption organisations.

Uncontinence

There was a fourth reaction in the children which was noticed by a considerable number of parents. At first, many children are restless, have bad dreams and sometimes start wetting their beds again – even though they were toilet-trained in the Home. Asian children appear to suffer from this more than European children. This is caused by the great changes the child has experienced. Bedwetting in older children is often caused by the great stress the child feels. All those new impressions and experiences raise this tension. The untrainedness may be long-term. In the first year, parents should not pay too much attention to possible untrainedness, particularly if the child is not bothered by it. When it lasts for a considerably longer time, well-known means (the pad and buzzer, a training programme and the like) can be brought in, if necessary in consultation with a paediatrician, a psychologist or an educationalist.

Are we now, from the various studies, capable of predicting serious adaptation problems which certain adoptive children will exhibit? To this I can wholeheartedly answer 'yes'. Children with a problematic background (long stay in a Home, various caregivers, abuse, etc) or a poor physical state when they arrive will always demand more attention and care than is considered normal for children of that age.

Finally, a remark about the first reactions of family members, neighbours and others. On the whole these reactions are of a positive nature, especially with

---

1   Almost the entire group from Thailand and their parents were approached again in 1992 and 1993. The report of this study will be published in due course.

parents for whom the adoptive child is their first child. The increase in contact with the neighbours is striking. They probably get to know each other better through the children and they also help each other with familiar problems such as baby-sitting. Especially since the neighbours can be very helpful, as well as unintentionally interfering, with respect to the child, parents would do well to give them explicit information concerning the peculiarities of the newcomer. An older child, for example, tends to be indiscriminate for a while in his or her demonstration of love. This hail-fellow-well-met person can, when he is denied something, easily go to the neighbours to get what he wants there. Therefore, neighbours and other relatives (living closeby) should be advised to take a somewhat neutral – yet kind and interested – position regarding the child initially, so that he will learn that he is treated differently at home. This way the child will learn more quickly what 'home' means. Mutual agreements with friends, family and, especially, the neighbours will often be necessary. In certain situations it can be useful to lend them some literature about behavioural problems with adoptive children. Neglected children can be very strongly inclined to manipulate their parents, even when they are only four or five years old. They tell stories that simply are not true. Usually these stories concern the food which the child supposedly does not get enough of or the spankings which are delivered. The imaginations of these children can be very rich. But, because of this, very sad situations can occur for adoptive parents. In my practice I have helped people who were, absolutely wrongfully, accused of abuse and neglect in such a plausible manner that the magistrate of a juvenile court had to intervene. Obviously these are (fortunately) extreme anecdotes, but many children exhibit a milder version of manipulative and testing behaviour. A fore-warned parent is fore-armed.

CHAPTER 5

The Adoptive Child at School

5.1 Comparison with peers

In several studies adoptive children have been mutually compared by country of origin and with Dutch peers.

I believe several noteworthy results have come up. It seems there are clear differences between European and non-European children. Adoptive parents are under the impression that European adoptive children differ little from other Dutch children. On the other hand, with non-European children, about 40 per cent of parents mention a visible advantage concerning independence, co-ordination and intelligence. Korean children, especially, appear to make a good impression on the parents as far as these are concerned. It is striking that many parents of Asian adoptive children assess their child higher as far as intelligence is concerned. This is probably because these children, as I have said before, were forced by the conditions in the Children's Home to generally behave more independently and be more skilful when handling appliances. Especially with young children this gives an impression of 'intelligence'. However, this mainly concerns 'practical intelligence'. In practice this does not say very much about the ability to learn abstract things.

Since the academic performance of the children was also compared, one was able to examine whether intelligent behaviour affected school performance. This is not the case. In fact, some of the children seem to lag behind, although the overall impression is that more than half of the children perform more or less equally as well as their peers.

5.2 Opinions of teachers

The teachers were also asked to compare the adoptive children with their classmates. These classmates are similar in socio-economic aspects. They come from approximately the same neighbourhood and, in any case, they go to the same school.

As for school performance, the children function reasonably well in general. Especially in reading, writing and language, they come through well in comparison with their classmates. Still, there are a few children who are obviously below average with regard to language performance; they often appear to have suffered from ear disorders. Most striking about this is that these children do have a satisfactory level according to the parents. Perhaps the positive opinion of the parents is due to the compensating factors I mentioned earlier. These make it appear as though they understand the language better than is actually the case. At school they do, however, get caught out – albeit not immediately. However, the opposite also occurs: the child's language performance is assessed as satisfactory at school but not by the parents. This particularly occurs in primary education. In some cases we see how the child suddenly does have problems with the various languages in secondary education. In retrospect, the parents were right – reason enough for us to ask teachers in primary education to critically review their opinion of the child if there is an obvious discrepancy between their judgement and that of the parents, especially when ear or eye disorders have been spotted. In any case, adoptive parents of children of two years of age and older need to be extra vigilant with regard to their children's language development. This also applies to teachers in primary education.

The subject of mathematics poses problems for more children and, on average, the performance level is lower than that of their classmates. Many parents mention that their child dislikes that subject in particular.

That adoptive children, with their very different backgrounds, achieve less at school is obvious to me. They simply do not come through well in comparison with children born, for example, in the Netherlands or Belgium. When, in the first years of their lives, the children are neglected, understimulated and left to themselves too much, it will usually have an effect on their cognitive performance later on and, therefore, on their performance at school.

It frequently seems that children who are older on arrival perform less well in all areas and have learning or concentration problems relatively more frequently. They also have more often re-sat a grade and they have to rely more on special types of education. Therefore, on the whole, parents need to pay extra attention to issues like concentration, language and numeracy problems, choice of school and the approach of the teachers. An educational method which pays more attention to the individual student is usually to be recommended for adoptive children. Placing the child in a class of 30 or more students brings with it many risks. At first it may seem that there are no problems, until it turns out that the child has hardly taken in any of the school material and is threatened with being transferred to a lower grade – and this while the child was just beginning to feel at home in this grade, on a social and emotional level. Important changes on a socio-emotional level are extra difficult for the (neglected) adoptive child. This child is particularly looking for security and safety.

This is why I advise adoptive parents against moving just after the (older) adoptive child has arrived. Sometimes holiday plans also need to be adapted. If the three-year-old toddler has been there for barely two months and the parents plan to go on a four-week holiday abroad, they would be asking for a much longer period of adaptation problems with the child.

Because of their great effort and involvement with their child, adoptive parents sometimes tend to overdo their help with schoolwork. What an adoptive child who, for instance, comes into the family as a three-year-old needs most is rest and time to get accustomed to all that which is new. To demand high cognitive achievements when the child goes to school a year later does not fit in with this. One's demands and desires have to be adjusted to the child's needs and abilities. It may be very sensible to keep the child in the first grades of primary education/nursery education for an extra year. These children often need extra time in order to prevent them from getting a negative assessment in front of the class. Due to their lack of basic feelings of safety and security, they are at risk of developing feelings of inferiority. After all, they continue to be the worst of all the students, they continually fall short in many respects and are often teased and ridiculed by some of their classmates. The adoptive child may even get strong feelings of guilt because the failures at school are blamed entirely on himself. On the rebound, the adoptive child may acquire very annoying habits in order to get the much sought-after attention and appreciation of classmates. He starts to steal all sorts of things – at first sweets to hand out, then money to buy a lot of sweets to give away and subsequently other things, like toys. This is how this child attempts to win his place within the group. It is possible for this 'stealing behaviour' to occur in all children, adopted or not. It is necessary for all children to feel safe and secure at school. However, if the child has had less opportunity to develop a normal conscience within the first few years of life, the chances of this 'socio-disturbed' behaviour are greater. For the child, it is not stealing but using what he needs from the abundance around him. We see this behaviour more frequently in adoptive children who are older on arrival.

Parents should, therefore, always confer with the teachers in question and give them all necessary information about the child. This consultation needs to take place regularly. The teacher needs to be shown that the child requires special attention. The parents can actually offer to give the child extra help with certain matters.

Does the preceding careful and attentive approach have a chance of success with these children in particular? On the whole, I think so. My positive assumption (exceptions excluded, of course) is, amongst other things, based on the teachers' opinion of the socio-emotional behaviour of the adoptive children at school.

We compared the 116 children from Thailand to classmates on four behavioural aspects by means of the *School Beoordelings Lijst* (School Assessment List). As far as the behavioural characteristics 'frankness' and 'sensitivity' are concerned there are hardly any differences, but there are differences with the aspects of work attitude and, especially, social contacts. The adoptive children appear to do better. I find it particularly interesting that the children with a problematic past (and therefore worse school performance) do better in work attitude than other adoptive children. They obviously do their very best at school. Once again this substantiates the general proposition of adoptive children from far-away countries, particularly children who have had to fight for survival during the first years of their lives and have learned that they have to stick up for themselves. These children are go-getters with a strong desire to adapt to all circumstances. Their zest for life is usually considerably higher than average.

According to the teachers, the adoptive children have better social contact with their classmates and the social integration of these children is better than that of the average Dutch child. Again, the children with an obvious problematic past do better. Although this is pleasing, I must make another comment: it is possible that the oft-mentioned positive discrimination of adoptive children plays a part and the teacher assesses the sweet-looking Asian child more positively than her classmates.

This is not the place to go into great detail about the various possible cognitive and/or emotional school problems of foreign adoptive children or how to deal with them. A great deal more information about the children is required. I have merely sketched a few outlines which came up as a result of several studies. Finally, I would like to point out one more important aspect. Let all adoptive parents keenly follow the performance of their child at school from the beginning (nursery school that is). Teachers often need to be fully informed and need to be guided when it concerns a foreign adoptive child who was, for instance, placed into the family as a two- or four-year-old. To assess this child by the same standards from the beginning may lead to the wrong conclusions. The child may, for instance, on the grounds of his co-ordination, strong vitality and social abilities be overestimated and thus receive too little of the specific attention which this child desperately needs. Also, a very neglected child may take years to come up to standard on a cognitive level – at least the standard of which the child is actually capable. The teacher needs to be patient and not judge too negatively. An intelligence test will not always yield a reliable decisive answer. The child can still not be compared to other children. First he must go through a longer period of recuperation. It is often more sensible to have an educationalist take a critical look at the developmental level of the child. If any deficiency is found, it will influence the learning capacity and cognitive maturity. In short, adoptive parents, and especially those who get a slightly older child (over 12 months), should follow their child's school life more actively than ordinary parents. They must understand that it can be a constant frustration for a child to be wrongly assessed and be in the wrong place at school. This may have negative consequences for the child's rehabilitation and could last for years to come.

CHAPTER 6

Some Years Later

6.1 Striking behaviour

To what extent are the children integrated into their families, at school and in other social circumstances after the first period of adjustment? Before reviewing the at times, very problematic behaviour of the children mentioned by parents, we need to put it into perspective.

Many children who grow up with their biological parents show behavioural problems from time to time. This simply goes with the development of children. Thus one may also expect all sorts of problems with raising adoptive children. The situation only becomes worrying when there are many more, other and difficult problems to deal with.

May we conclude from the research that adoptive children show signs of behavioural problems more often than other children? Should we compare foreign adoptive children with children born in our own country? I would like to answer this last question with an emphatic *no*. The normal situation in which a child grows up with his biological parents, and is well looked after by those parents, is in sharp contrast to the history of almost all adoptive children.

A child born in the Netherlands that is given up for adoption will first be placed on neutral ground for three months and will then definitively be taken on by the adoptive parents. In the meantime, the child has already experienced two separations and has possibly endured the negative effects of an unwanted pregnancy (it is known from research that stress from the mother during pregnancy can affect the child). A comparison with children from abroad is not easy to make. The conditions for Third World mothers who (have to) give up their child are usually very bad. I mention a few: shortage of food, a great deal of stress due to the chance of being cast out of the family and an unhealthy lifestyle. The girl may have tried an abortion, which may have damaged the child. For poor, unmarried mothers the delivery occurs with less help and the care for her and the child will subsequently be minimal. If the child then remains with the mother or other relatives for some time, it can be reasonably well taken care of. However, the chances are that when it is an unwanted child some, or more serious, negligence will take place right from the start. Many adoptive children end up in a Children's Home, with limited care facilities, for some time. In short, it is well known how physically and mentally hurt many of these foreign adoptive children are when they arrive in Europe or the USA. It would be highly surprising if these children did not show the negative consequences of this. Therefore, these children are not really comparable with a normal group of children. Does it make any sense at all to make comparisons? Yes, of course, for then adoptive parents are able to see which negative behavioural effects are to be expected and taken into consideration.

I shall briefly discuss some of the results of various studies so that aspirant adoptive parents are better able to take into account some of the particular behaviour which *might* be expected. I expressly say *might* because it is not always certain that a problematic background may have negative consequences. There are a few reasons for this:

- Often we know little about the child's background. For example, he or she may be two, three or four years old on arrival but in those first years was well looked after by the parents.

- Some children are simply less vulnerable than other children, they can take a lot more and seem to have a sort of inner defence mechanism.

- Some children are neglected and endure all sorts of traumatic events. For some time they show the negative behavioural consequences of their background but recover relatively quickly and reasonably well. What are considered to be adaptation problems, seem to be only that.

Research has shown that approximately one third of foreign adoptive children have developed a particular kind of behaviour or that it has not disappeared since the child's arrival. The most striking are: concentration and learning problems, overactive, prone to fighting, provocative behaviour, outbursts of anger, stuttering, having difficulty with sleeping somewhere else or going camping, stealing things, lying, bed-wetting, strong inhibitions and avoiding conflict situations at all costs.

All these problems need to be seen individually with respect to the entire family situation and the duration and frequency of the behaviour. Problems concerning emotional development are the most important. I will presently elaborate on this aspect, which is important for both parents and child.

All parents of the Thai children were asked whether they thought emotional development was normal as compared to peers, especially dealing with feelings, reactions when expressing emotions and emotional response to changes.

Approximately 10 per cent of the parents mention a dysfunction in dealing with feelings. As is to be expected, there is a clear connection with the age on arrival. In well over a third of the children who were over two years old on arrival, there is a dysfunction in dealing with feelings – in children less than seven months old on arrival this is only occasionally the case.

Reactions when expressing emotions is problematic for many more children (approximately 30%). When this occurs it often means a strong inhibition on the part of the child, and in several cases the parents mention a superficial manner of response. The behaviour very much resembles what we call 'everybody's friend' behaviour. With regard to other children with problems expressing emotions, several more or less individual abnormal behavioural patterns are mentioned (strong jealousy, fickleness, negative response towards either of the parents). Again, there is a clear connection with the age on arrival. The older the child is, the more often he will have problems expressing emotions.

It is remarkable that with parents with externally-oriented adoption motives, the children more often appear to have problems expressing their emotions. This can, amongst other things, be connected to the family make-up. It so happens that these parents often have biological children too. They will probably compare their adoptive child to their own child, something which childless parents are naturally unable to do.

In 5.2 (p.41) I mentioned something about the sensitivity to change in the neglected child. The parents of the Thai children were explicitly asked to assess the sensitivity of their child. As we suspected, it appears that a remarkably large group (30%) of Thai children do not respond normally to changes such as going on holiday, changing schools, going to another class at school or moving. This group includes 34 children. The parents of thirteen of them noticed an increase in feelings of insecurity and a further six couples mention patent anxiety reactions, especially at night. Five children responded with very withdrawn behaviour. The other ten children showed various abnormal response patterns, such as: highly passive behaviour, lack of initiative, direct resistance to changes, bed-wetting, excessive crying and an unstable temper.

Are these briefly-mentioned behavioural problems so serious that they are a burden to the parents? For a limited few (15%) this is indeed the case. Moreover, it appears to be mostly so with parents who had an older child on arrival. Apparently the behavioural problems of these children are much stronger than those of children who are younger on arrival.

The family composition leads to clear differences. The families with biological children often feel much more burdened with the problems. As a result of this, one would almost think that the capacity for coping in families with exclusively adoptive children is larger than in families with biological children. However, the latter families are, on average, larger. It is fairly obvious that larger families require more flexible parents.

There is another remarkable result. Parents who experience the behavioural problems of their child as a burden more often say that they had insufficient adoption information. From this one may conclude that good preparation has an influence on the way in which parents respond to possible problems. The better the parents are prepared, the less burdensome the problems. This conclusion is of great relevance to adoptive parents who get a child of approximately six months and over. These children more often show problematic behaviour such as lack of concentration, lying, stealing things (acting-out behaviour), 'everybody's friend' behaviour and emotional inaccessibility than children who arrived at a younger age.

The results of the Thai research discussed earlier correspond to the research conducted between 1988 and 1989 by the child psychiatrist, Verhulst, and the psychologist, Versluis-den Bieman at the Sophia Children's Hospital of Erasmus University in Rotterdam. They approached the parents of 3309 foreign adoptive children born between 1 January 1972 and 31 December 1975. Details were obtained of 2148 foreign adoptive children 10 to 15 years old (65% response). The parents were asked to fill in a questionnaire specifically meant for them, and a behaviour questionnaire for children aged between 4 and 16.[1] The data obtained were compared with a group of almost a thousand children of the same age from the south of Holland population. These data were gathered in 1983 in order to get an idea of the occurrence of behavioural problems in Dutch families. Two age categories were distinguished in order to get a better comparison and because of the internal difference: 10 and 11-year-olds versus 12 to 15-year-olds.

The researchers mention five points on which adoptive children differ strongly from the south of Holland group:

1. The higher percentage of problem children in both age categories of adoptive boys and in the group of adoptive girls of 12 to 15 years old. More than twice as many adoptive boys aged between 12 and 15 (23.0% vs. 10.3%) showed considerable behavioural problems.

2. Many children, especially boys between 12 and 15 years old were placed outside the home into residential institutions.

3. A high percentage of parents indicated a need for assistance for the behavioural problems of their child (16.1% vs. 2.6%).

4. There was a higher percentage of police/judicial contact in the year prior to the research of the adoptive group (1.8% vs. 0.4%).

5. Many adoptive children attend special education and appear to have school problems.

With respect to the nature of the behavioural problem, the adoptive boys and girls scored higher in the so-called 'externalising' dimension. This concerns socially undesired and annoying behaviour (vandalism, theft, hyper-activity, aggressive behaviour and such like). With the 12- to 15-year-old girls, the schizoid syndrome of the 'internalising' dimension occurred far more often too (7.1% vs. 2.2%). This

---

1　The Child Behaviour Checklist was used for this. It was developed by the American T.M. Achenbach and made suitable for Dutch use by Verhulst. It consists of 20 competence questions and 118 questions about behavioural problems. The questions were answered by the parents.

syndrome is characterised by strange, withdrawn and anxious behaviour. These parents cannot understand, let alone grasp, what is going on in their child. If this behaviour also coincides with aggressive, cruel or other anti-social behaviour, then it is understandable that the problems in the family may run high. Anti-social behaviour in their daughter appears to take place suddenly and without any reason.

6.2 Family problems may run high

By 1995 the Adoption Centre of the Utrecht University had had more than twenty years of practical experience in the treatment and counselling of adoptive parents, the adoptees themselves and the entire family. How difficult this can be has, in a manner of speaking, been personally experienced. Even though the adoptive parents are well-prepared and well-intentioned, and have a lot of attention and love for the newcomer, serious crises may still occur in the family. To illustrate this, I will give an example. This case was chosen because certain of the qualities and behaviour of the person concerned, as well as certain life-events, are quite general. Other literature also elaborately describes important personal examples. I refer to the book *Child of Other Parents* (Hoksbergen and Walenkamp 1991) in which Part 3 (entitled 'Personal Experiences') discusses five different cases from the perspectives of the adoptee himself, social workers and adoptive parents. The first part of the book by Geertje van Egmond (1987), the adoptive mother of a Colombian girl aged five on arrival, is also well worth reading.

Marjolijn

According to the documents, Marjolijn was eighteen months old when she first saw her new parents. They picked her up from India themselves. They had saved just enough money to do so. They had already started saving when they registered with an adoption organisation. For obscure reasons, they are unable to have any children of their own, although they want to have them very much. The mother's parents thought adoption a good idea, but the father's did not appear to be very interested. Marjolijn had already gone through a great deal during the first period of her life. When she was not even 12 months old a police officer found her on a rubbish dump near the station. He immediately took her to the nearest children's home in Bombay.

Marjolijn turned out to be quite under-nourished and had several festering wounds. She was also covered with lice. After a blood and urine test it appeared she had various vitamin and iron shortages. A particular worm type was wreaking havoc in her intestines. In short, Marjolijn's physical condition was poor. Since she had been brought at Christmas and the attendant who was in charge estimated Marjolijn to be 12 months old, based on her weight and height, her date of birth was filled in as '1–1–1970' on her new birth certificate. They called her Manya. Naturally the police did some questioning as to whose child she might be but it was like looking for a needle in a haystack.

Medically speaking, Marjolijn appeared to recover at the home. She interacted well with her first attendant, who was with her and 30 other little girls for approximately four months, but who was then unfortunately transferred to the boys' department. There was little Marjolijn's new attendant could tell the parents. Marjolijn ate well, at times she slept badly and she did not like hugging, also she cried remarkably often and did not seem to want to have much to do with the new attendant.

Marjolijn was entrusted to a Brussels family whom I will call Van Laerens. From the first encounter they tried to win her confidence. However, this was not easy as she hardly responded to her new parents. It appeared she did not wish to be caressed. She responded rather forcedly and rigidly when anyone tried to sit her on their laps. Nothing much changed in the first few months. However, in a medical respect it did: Marjolijn fully recovered and soon looked very healthy. Relatives, friends and acquaintances who saw her liked her very much. Her appetite was good, perhaps too good, she wolfed everything down. But, in all other respects, she remained stand-offish, even though the father felt it became less as far as he was concerned. Marjolijn's sleeping also remained restless. She had trouble falling asleep and often woke up screaming. After bearing it for a few weeks, and exhausted due to their own lack of sleep, the mother decided only to leave when Marjolijn was asleep. This helped, but every time she woke the screaming started again. Only when she slept with her parents did everyone get some rest. After approximately eight months they tried again to see whether Marjolijn was able to sleep alone, and miracle of miracles it worked.

After approximately two years, when Marjolijn was officially almost four years old, her parents believed that she felt reasonably well at home. Especially her behaviour with other children seemed normal.

They decided to adopt another child. Because this proceeded so much quicker, they were able to fetch a two-year-old boy from Calcutta within the year. They left Marjolijn at home with her grandparents because she had already stayed there a few times without any problems. Marjolijn also said that this was what she wanted. A few days after the parents had gone, the grandparents noticed that Marjolijn was very quiet. They had trouble getting through to her. She did what was expected of her, but she would not stand cuddling. Twice the grandmother had gone up at about eleven o'clock to see whether she was asleep yet, but this was not so. She looked up at grandmother with wide, frightened eyes. Two weeks later the family was re-united. Marjolijn's new little brother was called Redzun, which very much resembled his Indian name. The parents knew that with a child who had grown accustomed to his name it was better to hang on to it. During the first few months, Redzun required a lot of attention. At first Marjolijn responded very well to her little brother, but when it became obvious that he did not yet understand her very well, she gradually withdrew. Suddenly, the night-mares started again and she occasionally wet her bed. Furthermore, her desire for food appeared more unstoppable than before. The parents worried about this, even though the great amounts of food did not result in her gaining weight.

On the whole, she did well at school. At nursery school Marjolijn comfortably joined her classmates and at primary school she tried her very best. She was not a very bright pupil, but by carefully paying attention and making a good effort, she got pass marks. Therefore, the first school years passed by relatively calmly. Afterwards, looking back, the parents conclude that these were the quietest and best years. Still, Marjolijn always remained distant, especially towards her mother. There were no real expressions of love. The opposite was the case when you saw her with her dog (a cocker spaniel). The love was mutual and everyday her dog faithfully awaited her return from school.

When Marjolijn was in the fifth form, a good ten years old, she suddenly started to grow and physically quickly reached puberty. She was by far the first in her form and was teased considerably. Her parents were very surprised by the quick development and decided to have her age checked. Then it appeared that Marjolijn was probably almost one year older than was stated. At the same time, the quick hormonal development could be a reaction to the previous undernourishment. Her physical catching up happened very quickly during the first year after arrival: she grew approximately one-and-a-half centimetres per month. As a result of the early physical puberty, Marjolijn absolutely did not want to swim and did not like gymnastic (P.E.) lessons. This became less in the sixth form and completely disappeared when she went on to secondary education.

The parents noticed that Marjolijn never really asked anything about her past, although she did have books about India in her room which she read, as her parents knew. They discussed adoption matters with her but, since she obviously only listened and had no questions, they soon stopped doing that too. When she was approximately 13 years old, different and bigger problems arose. At school things were not going very well. She often got unsatisfactory marks, even though at first she still tried very hard. During this period the mother had a hard time. She was 48 (her husband was 49) and lost both her parents in the same year. The menopause had already awkwardly announced itself a few years earlier. She seriously suffered with the hormonal changes. All was well with the father and he had a promotion, which is why they could move to a much larger house just when Marjolijn was to start a new education. These changes had a somewhat annoying effect on Marjolijn. She was unbearable for months and hardly talked to her parents and brother. When she came back from school, she usually went straight up to her room. She passed with difficulty and her parents, who helped her a great deal, heaved a sigh of relief. In the second grade things suddenly became more difficult. She had trouble applying herself to her homework and was very preoccupied with herself. She gradually started to think of herself as small in comparison with her peers. Her growth had practically stopped. At home she tried out various hair-styles and clothes, much to the annoyance of her parents. They started criticising Marjolijn more and more. They also kept trying to get her to do her homework. In the course of the second year at school there were also complaints from the school. At times certain things disappeared, which were later found with Marjolijn. Her marks clearly fell back. Subsequently, she had to resit her grade. That year the holidays passed with difficulty for the entire family. Marjolijn went her own way as much as possible and avoided contact with her parents.

In the meantime, all went well with Redzun, but Marjolijn was very obstreperous. Her parents hardly had any hold on her. She did not say what she did and at times it turned out she was simply lying. She had a tendency to just say yes – even when it was no – and to give any answer which her parents would like to hear. During the holidays she also had her first serious boyfriend. The parents were not very happy about this, but any comment by them resulted in an outburst of anger. Marjolijn exploited her adoption status for the first time. When she was furious she would react by saying: 'My real mother would not have been this childish. I'll go back to India' and 'In fact you have nothing to say about me'. Her parents felt increasingly sad and insecure. An estrangement seemed to grow more and more, especially between mother and daughter. This was hardly surprising. The mother, who was socially active and had always maintained an almost full-time job, had completely different interests from her daughter. Marjolijn liked to fuss about her appearance, walk on very high heels – because then she seemed taller – and get boys' attention. For that matter, in certain things she was very independent for her fourteen years. She got a dress allowance and a food allowance for school, etc. However, she did not seem to find this enough. Her mother discovered that sometimes rather a lot of money had disappeared from her purse. She decided to be very careful not to leave money lying around and Redzun started complaining that from time to time he was missing some. Marjolijn categorically denied that she pinched the money. Then one day the school principal called with the embarrassing story that several children had seen Marjolijn emptying out pockets in the changing rooms. Partially because of the serious talks which followed, there was a terrible outburst. Marjolijn fled to her room, locked the door and, out of sheer anger, threw everything outside. Her parents were deeply embarrassed as the entire neighbourhood now knew that there were big problems within their family and they had managed to keep everything well hidden until now. They decided to seek advice from others.

First they got in touch with some good friends of theirs, by chance also adoptive parents. They advised them to put the family problems to a social worker, a psychologist or educationalist – one who, at any rate, also knew about adoption. However, within their circle of friends, the Van Laerens knew a well-known psychologist who worked from a psycho-analytical perspective and was prepared to take on the problems with their daughter. From that moment onwards, the family went through hell – which ended with Marjolijn running away to a shelter for runaway youngsters. She was then 15 years old and wanted nothing more to do with her parents. However, she could only stay at the shelter for a short time.

Since Marjolijn appeared to be very independent, it was decided that she could share lodgings with three other girls. All costs were to be paid by her parents. For months they did not see her at all. Her father called her at a particular time every week. Marjolijn was then very cool and distant, but her father believed that she found pleasure in talking with him. In the meantime, she had a steady boyfriend. She had completely given up on school and appeared to have no further interest in her dog. This period lasted for approximately two years. When Marjolijn was almost 18, things suddenly appeared to change. Although she had been coming home every weekend for some time, there was no in-depth conversation. On the contrary, her parents painstakingly avoided talking to her about serious matters unless she broached them herself. The psychologist had strongly suggested this aloofness.

Mrs. Van Laeren will never forget one particular day. It started off with an unexpected phone call from Marjolijn. Her boyfriend had suddenly dumped her for one of the other girls and, in the past two weeks, she had, by chance, also had extensive conversations with an eighteen-year-old adopted boy from Brazil. He had told her a lot about his troubles, especially with himself and his desire to know more about his real family. The boy felt very lonely, although his relationship with his parents was much better than Marjolijn's. Even so, he seriously contemplated suicide. He was very dissatisfied with his life and simply did not know what to do with it, what the whole point of living was. He felt a lot of hatred towards his birth parents, even though he knew that they would have wanted him to end up well; they had even sewn a picture of his birth mother into his coat. His adoptive parents had found it afterwards and given it to him.

Marjolijn suddenly realised that she was also at a turning point. She would have to try to make something of her life, to start studying again, find a good job, get on better with her parents and the rest of the family, and be less inclined to all sorts of short-term relationships with men.

She called her parents and got her mother on the phone. She asked whether she could come home that evening, then suddenly burst into a great crying fit. Her mother was so surprised that, at first, she did not know what to do. It was the first time she had heard her daughter like this. Then, on the phone, the mother said that she would come by immediately. She would cancel the lessons which she should have been giving that day…

6.3 What is to be learned from this?

Of course much more happened concerning Marjolijn's family than can be told here. I have only tried to outline an idea according to a few main points. Now, how should we look at all this?

First, Marjolijn is a very much wanted child, her new parents consciously want to devote themselves completely to her. They expect that, after a short period of adaptation problems, the child will soon feel at home – after all they want to open up all of their hearts to her, although the mother does go on working almost full-time and the father is clearly in the career stage. They do not realise that, for the first few years anyway, Marjolijn's arrival in itself is a full-time occupation. The parents have hardly prepared themselves for the arrival of an eighteen-months-old adoptive child. They have never read anything except the brochure of the mediating organisation. They are completely ignorant of how a child who was seriously neglected can have separation anxiety at the age of two (as became clear later) and how this child responds when she enters into an entirely new situation. They do not have any contact with other adoptive parents either. The adoption organisation is relatively small and has, at that time, little insight into the importance of mutual contact between adoptive parents.

In the short period of her existence in India – a good two years – Marjolijn developed several serious psychological disorders. Her birth parents, or whoever looked after her in the first few months, were hardly able to give her enough to eat and were not concerned with her, or not able to be concerned with her. This is apparent from the clear impairment in development and her medical condition (e.g. having eaten rotten food). At the Home she had several attendants, to whom she responded intensely. Arriving in Brussels she shows all the signs of suffering from separation anxiety. Because of a lack of basic trust and security, she is strongly curbed in expressing her feelings. There appears to be a mention of insensitivity (Hart-de Ruijter and Kamp 1972). Because of her experiences in India, she has become seriously frustrated in her 'instinctive' need of contact with attendants. She seems to be very withdrawn (apparently relatively many adoptive girls respond like this, according to the results of Verhulst), even though the vulnerability still remains. The relapse in non-toilet-trainedness which occurs with the arrival of her brother is clearly a reaction to the lack of attention from her mother. Supposing the mother had paid much more attention to the daughter, then maybe the tide could (quickly) have turned for the better at that stage.

Her parents wrongly believe that Marjolijn is not interested in her past. On the contrary, she would have wanted to hear much more, only she finds it difficult to show it. She has developed various fantasies which are partially of an aggressive nature. However, she does not direct this aggression onto anything specific. There is only a mention of acting-out behaviour when she is approximately 13 years old (clearly obstreperous, swearing, lying, experimenting with clothes, stealing things, etc). Then her parents no longer have any hold over her. Mind you, she almost completely cuts herself off from her mother; she is either in her room or out with her boyfriends or girlfriends. She also feels the attention given to her by her parents about her schoolwork, clothes and friends to be a great burden. In fact, she feels very lonely and unhappy with her own life. In a psychological sense, however, she is strong and dominant towards her peers. However, the latter is only show. She often tries to have her own way, blind to the emotional response of others. At times she has little social awareness. Subsequently the others almost all ignore her after some time. She is not easily frightened, as was to be expected. In India she survived situations from which most other children would have died quickly. Even so, Marjolijn appears to have more positive feelings towards her parents (for her mother too) than they think. If she is in deep trouble, she turns to them for support.

The parents have been in touch with the Adoption Centre since the year Marjolijn turned eighteen. Apart from several practical suggestions, such as taking part in various activities together and stimulating contact with peers (for instance through sport), we have also advised them to spend a holiday in India with her and to visit all the places which are of importance to their daughter. Naturally all this is in consultation with Marjolijn. It should be a mutual plan. Furthermore, we have suggested they get some literature about India and adoption for themselves and for Marjolijn.

At first, Marjolijn's response to the visit to India was very emotional – especially when she saw the place where she was found, which still looked very filthy. They managed to track down the police officer who had taken her to the Home. They also visited the Home. Details about children who had left more than ten years before had not been kept. When they arrived back home, Marjolijn initially did not wish to speak about the India experiences but after a few months she had an emotional outburst and then it became apparent that she had been worrying about her background for a long time, without her parents realising.

Now it is six years later. Marjolijn (24) has successfully finished a number of practical courses. She has her own lodgings but goes home almost every weekend. She still does not have a steady relationship with a boyfriend but she does have several valuable contacts with other adoptive youngsters. The experimental behaviour has by and large passed and there are few signs left of anti-social behaviour. She has a good job and is thus capable of completely looking after herself. Her parents look at her future with confidence. The only thing they regret is that Marjolijn and Redzun hardly have the need to stay in contact with each other and that Marjolijn has little contact with other relatives either.

6.4 Does it go wrong often?

Can we now come to a general conclusion about adoptions? In other words, does it often go wrong, or how often are there such serious problems as with the Van Laerens and what are the main causes? In the previously mentioned research, these questions have been answered from the position and qualities of the child. But is it also possible to point out important issues that have much more to do with the uniqueness of adoptive parenthood? I will now briefly say something about this.

Many adoptive parents start with feelings of insecurity about their own approach to the education and reactions of their child. This insecurity is often stronger when the child is somewhat older. The Thai research has illustrated that adoptive children over five or six months of age may show peculiar behaviour, let alone when a child of up to four years old, like Marjolijn, has been through traumatic experiences (such as divorce, accidents, the death of people who were important to the child or violent scenes). In short, the role adoptive parents fulfil when practising parenthood is certainly not equal to that of other parents.

The term 'role' is derived from sociology. It means: the set of standards, values and expectations one has towards people in a certain position. There is a distinction between position and situation role. A characteristic of a position role is that there are generally accepted standards and expectations of a person's behaviour in the relevant position or place within society – for instance, in the role of the parent, the adoptive parent or the teacher. However, with regard to the role of adoptive parent, the standards and expectations are not very clear as it is a relatively new phenomenon in our society – especially the role of parent of a foreign adoptive child.

Adoptive parents do then, by definition, have great uncertainties about their role as a parent. The development towards adulthood entails that everyone learns, usually via examples within one's own environment, how to deal with these uncertainties and important roles. For the role of adoptive parent of a foreign child, this process is initiated the moment that people contemplate adopting a child. Naturally, they have generally been presented with the parental role by means of a role model, for example via the upbringing by their own parents. However, we now know, from experience and various studies, that adoptive parenthood requires special qualities. For many reasons – including the relative obscurity of the role of adoptive parent – it is hardly surprising that there are, relatively speaking, more problems in adoptive families. Furthermore, recent studies have shown that the problems in adoptive families escalate higher than in other families, so that the child, the adolescent, needs to be placed outside the home either for a shorter or longer period of time. About the latter I will say some more here.

By means of an extensive inventory, it has been established that outplacement occurs in approximately five per cent of all adoptive families with a foreign child. A very important, perhaps the most important, cause is the child's complex negative experiences in the country of origin. Because the chance of this is simply greater as the child spends more time in the country of origin, we can see a direct and strong link between the age on arrival with the family and the chance of outplacement. Of all the children who are six and a half years or over on arrival, approximately 25 per cent will be admitted to a children's home. With children between one and a half and six and a half, this is approximately five to ten per cent. With children of up to six months old on arrival, it will be one per cent to one and a half per cent. Apparently, the start of puberty – when the child is approximately twelve years old – is a crisis period. On average, it is at that age that most children are placed outside the home for a shorter or longer period. Naturally, the problems have started earlier. For instance, the group of children under two and a half years on arrival develop serious problems when the children are approximately nine years old. The latter correlates with what is predicted according to theoretical opinions on identity development. Round about the age of ten, children become increasingly more aware of their own place – their identity

– within the family and society. They experience themselves more and more as a unique personality with, as time passes, a great continuity, for themselves as well as for people in their immediate environment. But, especially with adoptive children, this identity-shaping results in problems. In view of the manner in which they came into the family, this is simply to be expected. They lack the self-evidence of the natural alliance with the family. They have to, as it were, acquire their status and did not get it through any genealogical alliance.

The preceding may lead one to the incorrect conclusion that the causes for problems in adoptive families should mainly be sought in the behaviour of the children. The situation is much more complex. Thus, what is important are both factors connected to the parents and other relatives and the specific combination of the child and these parents.

Particularly in connection with this, I want to point out a very common pitfall: the often excessive and over-specific expectations of adoptive parents. Regularly, aspirant adoptive parents appear to make various concrete impressions about the child who is, as yet, unknown to them. All parents who are about to have a child do this, but the big difference for adoptive parents is that the child really is a complete stranger and has already had a certain history, of which the adoptive parents often know nothing. This has been extensively discussed in previous chapters. I am primarily concerned with the distinct warning that parents should not, as it were, burden the child with various expectations about how it should be and how it should behave. Neither will the arrival of the child increase the parents happiness substantially. Parents should accept the child as a unique individual; accept the way it is and respond flexibly to their child. To conclude, I will briefly mention a few pitfalls for parents:

- ° Sometimes parents are completely oblivious to the specific role of adoptive parent
- ° They are inadequately prepared
- ° They have far too high expectations
- ° They struggle with personal problems (not coming to terms with involuntary childlessness, bad youth experiences, etc)
- ° They are far too rigid in their approach towards the child.

Sometimes parents and child just do not hit it off. Sometimes this is manifest at the very first meeting. This 'not hitting it off', or 'wrong approach' makes it understandable that, with several outplacements in another family, there is, after some time, a much better family relationship.

The complexity of the educational situations in adoptive families makes it obvious that particular problems arise. Let it be clear that this only occurs in a limited amount of families. Success rates of 70 per cent to 90 per cent are repeatedly mentioned in adoption literature. But, what is success, and is failure its opposite? Naturally it is not as black and white as presumed in terms of success/failure. Anyway, when should one speak of failure? In an article in the newspaper *NRC* of 22 January 1994, I stated that perhaps 'we could consider failures all those adoptions which, according to adoptive parents and/or child, should in retrospect not have occurred'. This retrospective judgement can only be passed when the adoptee is fully adult, at least about 25 years old.

However, all this does not mean that many families have the need of pedagogical help at one point or another. Adoptive parents, like Marjolijn's parents, sometimes hesitate too long before calling for that help – sometimes so long that the problems reach a crisis and the only way out appears to be immediate outplacement of the child.

I would, therefore, urgently suggest that adoptive parents with problems of any nature seek assistance with institutions specialising in pedagogical/psychological problems within adoptive families. This could take the form of discussion groups for adoptive parents. I repeat my statement: 'Adoptive parents help adoptive parents best'. One could also think of social workers of adoption organisations, or general counselling institutions, the general practitioner and paediatrician and other authorities. Let all adoptive parents realise that things can go wrong in their family. They do not need to be perfect educators, even if they were once officially approved as adoptive parents. Timely and adequate intervention can prevent worse.

CHAPTER 7

Psychic Homelessness and Adoption[1]

7.1 Introduction

It might be thought surprising and striking that adoptive parents of foreign children so eagerly longing for one or more children often need professional assistance, or even residential care for their adoptive child. From research, we know the need for assistance is four to five times more often the case in adoptive families with a foreign child than in other families (Hoksbergen 1983; Geerars, 't Hart and Hoksbergen 1991).

In 1984–1986 there was much controversy in the Netherlands concerning the problematic side of inter-country adoption. According to a large study (Hoksbergen, Spaan and Waardenburg 1988), some interesting facts were found:

- Regardless of age on arrival, the highest rate of residential placement of inter-racial adoptees is reached when adolescence starts, that is around the age of 12 years. With boys, disruption starts, on average, nine months earlier than with girls.

- The older the child on arrival into the adoptive family, the higher are the chances that residential care will be needed. Of the group younger than six months old on arrival, about one per cent needs residential care and of the group over 6.6 years, about 20 per cent.

- Children from Asia or South America are three to four years younger at the time of residential care than adoptees born in Europe.

- With children younger than 2.6 years old on arrival, the first important problems (difficulties with interpersonal behaviour, acting out behaviour, interpersonal problems within the family, etc) appear around the age of nine years.

---

[1] A shorter and adapted version of this chapter has been published in: J.M. Abbarno (ed) 'Ethics of homelessness; Philosophical perspectives'. Rodopi Publishers, Value Inquiry Book Series, 1996.

An important factor behind these psychological problems of adoptive adolescents is, according to my experience, the feeling of being in-between two cultures and, more important perhaps, being in-between two families – the adoptive parents and the biological parents. I'll call this the 'feeling of psychic homelessness for the adoptive child'. How can we describe this phenomenon?

When someone says 'I have a home' or speaks of 'my home', the expression means that one feels secure under a certain roof, feels safe and has an obvious emotional bond with that home and the people who live there. Nancy Newton Verrier (1993) gives many significant examples in her book *The Primal Wound*. The title is expressing what many adoptees feel – the feeling that a part of themselves is missing or that they are experiencing a big empty hole inside. Many adoptees told Nancy that, no matter how close they are to their adoptive parents, there is a space reserved for the mother who gave birth.

Would social psychology be of any help in understanding this phenomenon?

In social psychological terms we are talking about the in-group or reference group, the group with which the person identifies, with which one has satisfying relationships and whose norms and values, to a certain extent, become one's own. Krech, Crutchfield and Ballachey (1962) define the reference group as:

> Any group with which an individual identifies himself such that he tends to use the group as a standard for self-evaluation and as a source of his personal values and goals. The reference groups of the individual may include both membership groups and groups to which he aspires to belong. (p.102)

I'll limit myself here to the relationship between the adoptee and the adoptive and biological family. Both groups are what I call 'micro reference groups from the adoptee's perspective'. The adoptive family is the most important micro reference group for the adoptee for an extensive period. As the adoptee grows up, the biological family turns out to have an important 'reference' function as well. Sometimes this is the reference group 'to which one aspires to belong'. This can become apparent from all sorts of fantasies, but also from concrete actions. Think of questions that the child asks, and the information acquired! Do motives for searching not stem from this 'aspiring to belong'? An adopted child gets (adoptive) parents who want to have a child and who are desperately longing to welcome him or her in their home and heart; to give their new family member all the safety, sense of security, attention, and love that he or she needs.

This is quite different from what was generally the case with what we, in Europe, call 'the homeless' (people without any psychological and/or physical settlement, for example, when they were young). It appears, from research in the Netherlands, that those who are homeless were often neglected in their youth and were unwanted and rejected in the first years of their lives. Seventy per cent of the homeless have spent some time in Children's Homes. They experienced too little safety, love and security with their biological parents; early childhood neglect is one common characteristic. These grow into people who, due to psychological reasons (not due to cognitive reasons), are not able to live and function independently in society. From a lot of research and the hard demands of society, we understand why characteristics of the homeless indicate that these people hardly have any chance in society. They have a fundamental distrust of themselves and others and, because of this, they cannot easily develop normal relationships. Homeless persons experience intimate emotional bonds as a threat and are not able to deal with emotional processes. They also show a lack of sense of identity, evidenced by limited insight into one's own possibilities, muddling of fantasy and reality, insufficient impulse control, great need for attention, amoral behaviour and fear of failure – sometimes combined with high demands of self. They are very often strongly manipulative and they show externalised problem behaviour such as stealing, sexual provocation and vandalism. Their limited planning ability leads them to live from day to day. The homeless are people who often combine their feelings of psychic homelessness with physical homelessness. They are insecurely bonded and often have a high measure of animosity towards their environment. This picture is undoubtedly very similar to that in the United States.

7.2 Homelessness and inter-country adoption

If home-life circumstances for adopted children is relatively favourable, must we give them special care and attention? In short, is psychic homelessness such a frequently occurring phenomenon for adoptees that crucial measures must be taken to assist those adoptees who suffer from it? Looking at some of my research results I have to confirm this question.

Many before me in the United States, such as Jane Paton (1954), Anna Fischer (1973), Betty Jean Lifton (1975, 1979), Arthur Sorosky, Annette Baran and Reuben Pannor (1984), Nance Verrier (1993), and so many others, have repeatedly and thoroughly demonstrated that adoptees need this special care.

What I am concerned with here is homelessness in the psychological sense; with *psychic homelessness*. By this I mean: the experience of not completely belonging in the family in which one is growing up, that is, in which one spends most of one's youth. This causes insufficient bonding and a feeling of rootlessness. For inter-country and/or inter-racially adopted children, an added aspect is that of feeling torn between two cultures, of having two ethnic identities, of being 'in-between' people (Tahk 1986). This feeling of being 'in-between', however, can be found to a certain extent in all adoptees, regardless of their race. For this reason, I have distinguished between being culturally in-between and being emotionally in-between. In my opinion, being emotionally in-between applies to all adoptees to different extents.

One of the consequences of this complex experience of social reality can be that the nearest micro reference group (the adoptive family) has a weaker, and possibly ambivalent, identification function for the adoptee. Some adopted children will experience a strong sense of homelessness, and others will not have such strong feelings. Important life experiences, such as having one's own children or death of parents, have a large influence on this sense of homelessness. One should take into consideration that homelessness or feelings of being torn out by the roots are characteristic across different groups.

People who grow up in a completely different family from the one they were born into (Dutch adoptees), or even originate from a completely different region or ethnic group of the population (inter-country adoptees), will often experience a certain measure of psychic homelessness.

Inter-country adoption has become a world-wide phenomenon that is closely related to important historical events. It essentially developed after the Second World War. As a consequence, many orphans from Germany and Austria were moved, especially to the United States. The removal of mixed-race children from South Korea and Vietnam in the 1960s and 1970s was known as the babylift during the last days of the war from Saigon to the United States in 1975. Many mixed-race children, mostly from South Korea, also came to European countries.

Over the past decades, television has kept us up to date on disasters, which, time and again, move married couples to open their homes to adoption. By way of a spontaneous expression of involvement in the needs of the children of disasters, these married couples are willing to receive one child into their families. Recently, this has been the case with the children of Bosnian women who had been raped.

In this way, adoption of children from South Korea was started in 1969, and by 1994 there were 3793 South Korean children in the Netherlands and about 100,000 in the United States.

Since 1975, some 800 to 1000 children have been adopted annually by Dutch families (Table 7.1). In 1994, 23 countries were involved – among which, the most important are: Columbia, China, Sri Lanka, India and Brazil (Table 7.2). Although, in this context, there exist no international statistics, approximately 25,000 children annually, mainly from Asia and South America, go to the West for adoption. The United States accounts for as many as 10,000 foreign adoptions each year (Bachrach *et al.* 1990).

7.3 An example

In the summer of 1962, I was faced with rootlessness for the first time. I returned from New Guinea in June, having spent a year there on voluntary service. To spend the months before starting my studies at the university usefully, I decided to go to an Austrian work camp of the, then, European Working Community for Youth. There were also students from the United Kingdom in the camp. We helped to close the last barracks for refugees from World War II. One of my jobs was to visit the less able-bodied inhabitants of the barracks to persuade them to attend the meetings we had organised. In this way, I met men from different backgrounds and circumstances. But above all, I was a witness to the great effects that being

Table 7.1. Dutch and foreign children placed for adoption 1970–1994

Year	Dutch Ad.Child	Foreign Ad.Child	Total Placed Ad.Child	Total by Lawyer Assigned Adoptions	Total Born Alive Child	Step-Parent Ad.
			incl.'56–'69	6877		
1970	747	142	889	1209	238.912	
1971	568	159	727	1155	227.912	
1972	396	203	599	1292	214.133	
1973	328	316	644	1260	194.993	
1974	214	619	833	1679	185.982	
1975	171	1018	1189	1535	177.876	
1976	157	1125	1282	1492	177.090	
1977	142	1105	1247	1720	173.296	
1978	144	1211	1355	1544	175.400	
1979	143	1287	1430	1798	175.000	
1980	104	1594	1698	1901[1]	181.300	106
1981	99	1161	1260	2543	178.600	518
1982	77	1045	1122	2365	172.070	559
1983	66	1365	1431	1937	170.240	535
1984	63	1099	1162	1840	174.440	462
1985	72	1137	1209	1619	177.000	356
1986	63	1292	1355	1781	184.300	365
1987	39	872	911	1963	186.676	367
1988	49	577	626	1629	186.647	408
1989	30	642	672	1265	188.979	372
1990	52	830	882	1174	197.965	415
1991	49	819	868	1338	198.665	359
1992	42	618	660	1451	196.734	356
1993	42	574	616	1275	195.748	396
1994[2]	45	594	639	1120	195.611	377
	3,902	**21,404**	**25,306**	**46,762**		**5,951**

Notes:

1 Including the step-parent adoptions 1980 and following years; law has force since 1979.

2 Number of Dutch adoptees is an estimation

Source: Central Office of Statistics.

Table 7.2. Most important countries for inter-country adoptions in the Netherlands 1970–1994

Country	Number of Adoptions					Total
	1990	1991	1992	1993	1994	Number

Total number of adoptions to 1990 is 17,969

Country	1990	1991	1992	1993	1994	Total Number
Austria	–	–	–	–	–	291
Bangladesh	–	–	–	–	–	495
Bolivia	1	–	3	1	–	6
Brazil	91	111	57	72	67	776
Chile	2	3	–	1	–	203
China	–	–	26	29	75	130
Colombia	208	169	181	146	125	3395
Costa Rica	1	10	–	–	–	54
Dominican Republic	1	2	–	–	–	46
Ethiopia	33	33	49	41	40	270
Germany	–	–	–	–	–	97
Greece[1]	–	–	–	–	–	576
Guatemala	3	3	1	–	1	9
Haiti	19	–	12	8	32	244
Hungary	3	5	4	5	6	29
India	92	77	71	65	51	2552
Indonesia	–	–	–	–	–	3071
Israel	3	3	3	3	1	18
Jordan	–	–	5	22	–	27
Korea	6	9	11	4	27	3793
Lebanon	–	1	–	–	–	327
Mauritius	–	–	–	–	–	52
Peru	4	6	–	2	–	186
Philippines	13	12	10	10	4	152
Poland	22	40	29	29	20	188
Romania	4	23	2	3	7	40
Sierra Leone	4	1	5	–	–	11
Sri Lanka	263	228	97	62	73	3263
Surinam	17	25	9	8	13	126
Taiwan	17	31	23	27	19	182
Thailand	19	23	17	23	19	295
Yugoslavia	–	–	–	–	–	82
Others[2]	4	4	3	13	14	418
Total	**830**	**819**	**618**	**574**	**594**	**21,404**

Notes: 1 Most adoptions before 1970

2 Up to 1974 included countries mentioned above, which means that the number of adoptions from Germany, Austria and Yugoslavia will probably be higher.

Source: Ministry of Justice, The Netherlands.

uprooted from family and country can have on a person. A considerable number of children were relinquished for adoption. Several thousands of these children moved to other European countries and to the United States.

An extreme example of being uprooted that I will never forget is that of a former rich bank director from the south of Hungary, a territory where the German population used to have a lot of influence. This German-speaking man had lived in barracks for 17 years, was unemployed and had been without family for the last 14 years. His wife had run off with another barracks inhabitant. His two children had abandoned him many years ago. When I entered his room, I found him sitting on the floor in the middle of the room as usual. He looked dazed and apathic when he saw me. In fact, this 60-year-old man was already demented. Almost from the beginning, this man had not been able to get over the fact that he had lost his home and his health and that his wife and children had deserted him.

This example may not seem directly related to the people we are especially concerned with here. Since the man was already 43 years of age when he was driven away from his home, there is no question of adoption. Yet the consequences are quite extreme. I give this example to show the serious effects that psychic homelessness can have on people and why we must learn how to prevent it. It affects many groups of people, for example:

○ People born of an unwed mother who grow up in a Children's Home and, later on, as step-children or foster-children. Some of these people have no idea who their biological parents are. In the Netherlands an increasing number of people are rebelling against secrecy. Among them is Riet Monteyne, a woman in her forties, who, in 1989, conducted a 31-day hunger strike to prevent the destruction of files, among which were her own, with background information on children who had lived in Children's Homes. In 1992, a middle-aged woman, whose mother refuses to tell her who her father is, filed a law-suit against her mother. This was the first court case with such a charge. It has been postponed 17 times.

○ Those people who grow up with the mother's side of the family but do not know the identity of their father. In some cases even the mother does not know (any more) who the father was. Think of the increasing numbers of those born by artificial insemination and in-vitro-fertilization. This whole group consists of nearly five per cent of all births. A special group concerns divorced couples. The care-taking parent, usually the mother, wants nothing more to do with her ex-husband. For her children, her ex-husband is a non-person – even though he is their father. Later in life, during adolescence or adulthood, many of these children start searching for their other parent – who has often been described in harsh terms.

○ The population which is the subject of this book is the group of fully
    adopted people of Dutch or foreign origin. In 1993, there were
    approximately 20,000 adoptive children of Dutch origin and
    approximately 21,000 adoptive children of foreign origin.
    Abandonment of children has almost completely disappeared in
    countries like the Netherlands, Belgium and Scandinavia – since 1970
    there has been a steady yearly decrease in the number of children put up
    for adoption and since 1982 only 2 to 5 children per 1 million
    inhabitants were up for adoption. In the United States (and in almost all
    other countries) this number is much higher, although the exact
    numbers since 1975 are not available (Pierce and Vitillo 1991).

○ Other historical examples of homeless groups include children of the
    German or Japanese occupation and of our liberators in 1945, an
    estimated 10,000 people. Over 2,000 Jewish foster-children who
    survived the war sometimes had to go from hand to hand. Think also of
    the 400 orphans from Dutch parents living in Indonesia who did not
    survive the Japanese concentration camps (Keilson 1979; ICODO 1992).

7.4 Causes of psychic homelessness

I have explained above what I mean by homelessness and its relation to psychic
homelessness. If we look at the first period of foreign adopted children's lives, we
must ask the question: 'To what extent does affective neglect and being unwanted
lead to feelings of psychic homelessness during adolescence and in adulthood?'.

Can we assume that children who were affectively neglected during the first
two months after birth or during the first few years, and who were not able to
develop an explicit attachment to their parents, literally and figuratively do not
feel at home in this world? That they feel like 'strangers' among people? Which
aspects of their lives lead adoptees to identity problems and feelings of psychic
homelessness?

The *age and health condition during placement* of these children are important
factors (Hoksbergen, Spaan and Waardenburg 1988). If we look at the *situation at
the time of arrival* of children six months and older, we can state that the majority
of these children have been neglected psychologically or physically. Some have
also been abused and maltreated. With these children, we observe a pattern of
behaviour that can cause great difficulties for the adoptive parents. Because of
their experienced lack of safety and security, older children often distrust all adults.
This can be manifested by an inability to bond. The child has a lot of difficulty
binding and feeling safe with his new parents. Behaviour that is strongly aversive,
avoiding and being everybody's friend, are symptoms that label these children's
attitudes as socially disturbed. In the Netherlands and Belgium the term 'bottomless pit syndrome' (Egmond 1987) is often used as a short indication of social-

emotional disturbed behaviour. When further specifying what this means, however, we miss the experience of psychic homelessness.

The Belgian Association for Parents of Bottomless Pit Syndrome Children in its Tri-monthly Magazine *What Now* clearly sums up the symptoms of the syndrome:

1. There is no real *base* to the existence. It is just like a bottomless pit! You put endless amounts of love, attention and care into it but seldom get anything back.

2. The syndrome often appears in older adoptive children whose past history is insufficiently known. But it appears just as often in natural children, foster-children, or step-children, who, for some reason, lacked basic trust in their parent(s).

3. There is little or no ego and no trust in adults, and, as a result of this, there is a deeply-rooted fear of establishing solid relationships. There is a strong tendency to make multiple contacts. Because of this, it is difficult for such children to sense the problems of others.

4. They experience the intimate emotional bonds within the family as a threat. There is more appreciation for the shallow attention from many others than for the personally-aimed attention from a few dependable persons. There is a constant struggle for power between the care-giving parent(s) and the child, a struggle that is not perceptible for outsiders. Besides, the child is able to turn emotions on and off as if on command.

5. The devastation caused by the earliest experiences of 'pain' or 'being unwanted' staggers belief. This lack of basic trust during the very first years of life often expresses itself in the urge to be destructive of self or those nearest (parents). Other expressions of this aggression can be cruelty towards animals, vandalism, insomnia, provocative sexual behaviour and running away. Usually one sees an insatiable hunger for attention.

6. Brakes or thresholds are practically non-existent in the child. The development of the conscience did not get a good start.

7. The child exhibits survival behaviour and apparent adjustment. The child is a genius at observing, assessing and manipulating those around him. There is a strong tendency to play both parents and other family members off against each other.

8. The child continually feels frustrated.

9. The child has relatively little sense of time and space. Learning disabilities often arise, despite normal intelligence.

10. The initial phase is usually characterised by incredibly well-adjusted behaviour, without homesickness. Over time, the behaviour towards the care-giving parent(s) becomes more and more rejective. The initial behaviour, however, is maintained towards others – sometimes even towards the parent who does not directly take care of the child.

The diagnostic survey of children with bottomless pit syndrome almost completely corresponds with what Keilson (1979) concludes in his research on 204 Jewish foster-children. In the group of children who were under four years of age at the time they were separated from their parents (71 children), but also frequently in older age categories, Keilson most often observed neurotic effects on character. That is to say that there is a possible neurosis (non-malicious, mild form of a psycho-social disorder) that is deeply anchored in the person and, therefore, difficult to cure. Symptoms are: great insecurity, contact disorders, paranoid attitude and psychopathiform conduct disorders. This last term was introduced by Hart de Ruijter and Kamp (1972). It is about behaviour that bothers the child, but that is especially experienced as disturbing or unpleasant by the environment. It is mainly aimed towards the outside world (acting-out). Violent and primitive aggressive impulses against the outside world are apparently indulged in an uninhibited fashion, and guilt feelings seem to be practically non-existent (de Witte 1990). The microreference group can also belong to this outside world. Likewise, Keilson saw, in his Jewish group, significant loyalty and identity problems that can lead to serious crises, especially during adolescence. Many Jewish children were placed with childless married couples. This offers strong support to the hypothesis that children who were neglected at a young age will often experience psychic homelessness later in life – that is, they have problems with bonding and feeling attached. If they show this at all, they often do so in a neurotic fashion – a way that is not realistic.

We can read about examples of these unrealistic emotional feelings in the theme issue *Jewish children who went underground back then* of the Dutch organisation for help of victims of war ICODO (1992). Emmy Kolodny, who was born in 1939, went into hiding in several households between 1943 and 1945 and returned to her mother (her father had been murdered). When she was an adult, she first moved to Israel and then to the United States. She later wrote an article entitled *Who am I?*. She ends her story with the following:

I do not feel as if I ever found a home. When we were children we were always told that we had to be grateful, because we had others to thank for our lives. 'You are lucky to be alive' was something we heard often. Ever since 1945, when we came 'home', I have lived with feelings of guilt that I survived the persecution. To this day I feel the pressure of the yoke on my shoulders of the unwanted responsibility for the fact that I am alive.

7.5 The story of Peter – an inter-racial adoptee

Peter is a typical example of an adopted child who experiences psychic homelessness. Peter did not really feel at home in the Netherlands. Where his acting-out behaviour is concerned, he is an extreme example, but, in my opinion, he is a genuine representative of the psychic homelessness of some (foreign) adoptive children.

Peter is the son of a European father and a black mother. At the age of six, he came from a foreign country with his three-year-old brother to his childless Dutch adoptive parents. He lived at different addresses in his country of origin but had no negative memories of his mother. He never knew his biological father. After the normal period of adjustment, Peter behaved himself reasonably well. He appeared to address himself quite intensely to his father. Socially speaking, things went well too, although at school he had a hard time keeping up. His language development began to lag behind and he was barely able to finish a technical training. Peter is quite closed by nature but, until his twentieth birthday, he fared reasonably well. His parents had no complaints about him. He was honest, diligent, trustworthy and had a good relationship with his father, who is very fond of him. Later on, however, his father would tell me that he never had the feeling that he could see through him completely. Sometimes a wall seemed to exist between Peter and the outside world. Peter had no friends. The adoption subject is somewhat problematic in this family. The fact that their children might have problems concerning their adoption status seems to elude the parents. For years Peter seemed unwilling to talk about adoption. It does, however, strike his parents that, as Peter grew older, more and more objects and articles from his country of origin appear in his room. He also withdrew into himself more often. He had a girlfriend, but he did not discuss his background with her.

When his parents approached me, things had gone seriously wrong with Peter. The process of withdrawal had become of a sickly nature. It is likely that certain very disagreeable facts had furthered this process. His brother had run away and had more or less got into trouble. Peter was not able to find a good job, which was very likely due mainly to discrimination. People called him names on the street. His limited knowledge frustrated him as well. The first time I approached him, communication was only possible by way of notes that he handed to me in silence. As a matter of fact, neither his parents nor I were able to see much of him at all. Dinner had to be put in front of his door at times. It had been like this for several weeks. One day, things took a turn for the worse. He suffered from a complete blackout and, in that state, he seriously threatened his parents.

Peter had to be admitted into a psychiatric clinic involuntarily. After a week, I visited him at his request. He wanted to know more about his background, about his biological parents and about the reason why he was relinquished for adoption. He wanted to emigrate to his country of origin. He claimed he did not feel like a Dutchman or have a bond with his parents. He wanted to leave the clinic as soon as possible. Peter found it ridiculous to be locked up and he did not feel at home with the other patients. He wanted to track down his biological family and told me frankly that he only felt bound to his unknown background and that he had always felt this way.

He felt strongly about his father, but saw him more as a friend. He found his adoptive mother important as a practical care-giver and not as a mother. The way Peter saw it, his mother lived far away.

By the time Peter was discharged from the clinic, it was possible, together with his girlfriend, to make his dream come true and find his biological parents. He stayed away for two months and travelled around the country trying to find information on his relatives. However, he did not succeed. But he did gain insight into his situation as a little boy as the last Children's Home he lived in still existed. Following an extensive conversation with Peter a few weeks after his return, I reached several conclusions:

1. The mystique of his country of origin had disappeared. Peter now talked about it in realistic terms in a both negative and positive way. He wanted to visit the country more often but did not want to emigrate there.

2. He had become calmer and seemed more or less to accept his place in our country. He planned to move somewhere else and live independently.

3. He had told his adoptive parents all about his trip. His relationship with them had normalised.

4. It frustrated him tremendously that he had not been able to find out anything about his relatives. He planned to continue his painstaking search through the useful contacts he had established.

Finally, he came into contact with a somewhat older sister who had been adopted in Europe as well. They did not know about each other's adoptions.

Towards the end of 1995, three years later, Peter has visited his country of origin, found some relatives and has also found suitable employment. There is no more question of psychotic behaviour. He is more communicative and the relationship with his parents has normalised. He lives in Belgium with his brother, who has the same biological parents and has been adopted by the same adoptive parents as Peter. Peter's feelings of not completely belonging have diminished but have not disappeared. He still does not feel like he is the real son of his adoptive parents, nor does he feel completely Dutch. The positive part of the story is that Peter has learned to live with the peculiarities of his life.

7.6 The need for specialised after-care

Adoptive parents will hopefully obtain more information on the effects of neglect and abuse that develop into serious forms of psychic homelessness. Hopefully we will be able to advise parents on how to deal with some conduct disorders caused by neglect during early childhood while they adjust to adoption status. The conduct disorders can be significant. Just like the physically homeless, adopted children placed-out-of-home show, for instance, a strong tendency towards aggression. On the items 'stealing' and 'fighting' on the Child Behaviour Checklist they scored respectively 12 and 10 times higher than the control group (Geerars, 't Hart and Hoksbergen 1991). The chance of becoming lonely is such an obvious characteristic of the homeless and ranked high in their responses. For instance, no less than a quarter of these youths have any contact with the adoptive family. Moreover, if we bear in mind that one can assume that adoptive children generally have less contact with other family members, the chance of psychic and physical homelessness is great.

The chance of isolation is greater for adoptees than for other people. We should realise that it is the married couple who chose adoption and scarcely ever the rest of the family. There is no self-evident and socially obliging bond between relatives. This can be established if the other relatives admit the adoptee into their midst as a family member. One condition for this is that the adoptee and the family are able to get along. It is safe to assume that when there are big family problems from the moment the adoptive child arrives, the chances of 'getting along' with the rest of the family are slim, whilst the chance for what I call 'adoption-isolation' is great.

In the above there is no mention of the fact that some adoptees can really experience great support from just that one relative with whom they get along well, despite the possibly great problems with the adoptive parents. Likewise, we should think of the loyalty problem adoptees have – the problem where they have feelings towards two sets of parents, while the parents with whom they grow up can feel this as threatening to their parenthood. Adoptees often realise this and try to take up a loyal position. This is one of the reasons why some adoptees only start the search for their biological family after their adoptive parents have died. It is likely that this loyalty problem is also closely related to the phenomenon of psychic homelessness. I advise adoptees who are in doubt, to search.

7.7 Searching

I assume that the feelings of psychic homelessness are closely connected with the motives for searching. This is precisely what we see in the life of our adoptee Peter and what 20-year-old Rita tells us before she leaves for Nepal to meet her biological mother: 'I think that I will only be able to settle down once I see her again'. But Rita was already 9 years old when she came to live with her adoptive parents. Maricella, 15 years old, visits her country of origin, Guatemala, with her adoptive-father. After the first intense emotions of seeing the familiar places that she left seven years before, she has to admit that she has become a stranger in Guatemala too, although she says 'she feels more at home' there (Trouw 1988).

Over the last few years the media have regularly publicised stories of youths or adults who found either one or both of their parents again. Throughout all the stories and examples I have presented, some characteristics of the situation become clear:

First, the effects are irrespective of the person's character and dependent on one's life experience, the relationship with the adoptive parents, how the experience of adoption status is felt and on the reaction of one's biological parents. Sometimes there are therapeutically intended effects: one wants to meet a blood-relation and is searching for one's own identity. The need can be great and the satisfaction thereof can bring a certain calm. However, when the search is only partially successful, or if entirely unsuccessful, new psychological problems, such as confusion and, perhaps, feelings of abandonment, emerge. This is the case where a traced biological parent refuses any contact. This risk exists and I recommend using a professional intermediary. A certain amount of follow-up care is also recommended.

Research has shown that most encounters go well, but the expectations and behaviour of the adoptees are very different from those of the biological parent(s) and, therefore, in most cases the effects of meeting each other are different as well. The search is, in itself, an active process of coming to terms with one's own identity. If, for the adoptee, one can compare adoption to post traumatic stress disorder, then there can be a necessity for searching in order to gain control over negative symptoms. According to DSM-III-R (1987), the essential feature of post traumatic stress disorder is that some characteristics (fears, nightmares, over-sensitivity to sounds, dreams, perception disorders, and others) develop as a consequence of events that one experiences as traumatic.

My last finding is that encounters with, or a visit to, the country of one's origin can stimulate one to learn to live with the generation break and with feeling 'in-between'.

7.8 To conclude

In 1987, when Aruna Bandling was 21 years old, she started the search for her mother in India. As a six-year-old, she came from a Children's Home in Bombay to a young Swedish couple. Her answer to the question of whether she herself as Swedish or Indian, is: 'I am not Swedish, I am not Indian, I am nothing' (Foreign Adoption 1987).

Such a reaction may seem extreme, but I am afraid that it is the heart of the matter. Adoptive children can run into big problems with their identity, and with receiving a satisfactory answer to questions such as: 'Who am I actually?'; 'Who am I in your eyes?'; 'Am I still the same person I was before the adoption?'. For many children (foreign) adoption seems to be the only solution. These children, however, do not remain children. As adolescents, and later on as adults, they confront us with new problems, of which the solution or improvement are again of vital importance.

I see several responsibilities. Diminishing the adoptees' feelings of psychic homelessness is a great responsibility for the biological parents, the adoptive couple or the social worker – for only then can the adoptee feel more at home in his social surroundings.

Society carries a great responsibility as well. An adoptive system built on sentimentality and secrecy, that too often pits birth and adoptive parents against each other and is unable to acknowledge the simple human right of adoptees to have access to their own life-history is also a main reason for feelings of psychic homelessness for so many adoptees. Let us fight for adoptees in the USA to have the same rights and opportunities as other human beings.

CHAPTER 8

Trans-Racial Adoption and Discrimination

8.1 Is trans-racial adoption in the best interests of the child?

In this chapter I'll first briefly deal with policy and principles around trans-racial adoption. Then I'll say more about the results of some research and experiences from our clinical practice.

First, we have to realise that in the Netherlands, in contrast with the USA and Great Britain, the discussion about trans-racial adoption has not been influenced by a situation where a considerable number of children in care are of an Asian, African or South American background. Children of ethnic backgrounds, living in the Netherlands now, were born in other countries – Asia, Africa or South America – in the Netherlands, the Scandinavian countries, Belgium and other European countries there has never been any policy to restrict, or even stop, trans-racial adoptions. Foreign and trans-racial adoption is, for instance in Holland and Sweden, almost the only way to be able to adopt a child. As I have said before, the surrender of children born in those countries hardly exists anymore. No more than about 2 to 4 children per million of inhabitants are relinquished for adoption. In the USA and Great Britain these figures are much higher. In the USA you have to think of 150 to 200 children per million of inhabitants (Flango and Flango 1995), and in Great Britain of about 50 children (Hall 1986).

In the last twenty to twenty-five years in most West European countries, with the exception of Great Britain, adoption of a child means adoption of an Asian, South American or, sometimes, African child. So, almost from the beginning, foreign adoption has been primarily trans-racial adoption. There was hardly any discussion as to whether these children were better off with parents of the same race simply because these people hardly exist in these European countries and we were never speaking of black children from institutions inside Holland. Trans-racial adoption means adoption of a child from another country, often a parentless child in need of loving parents somewhere on earth. In several ways, however, the principle that the ethnic background of an adoptee should influence the placement policy of adoption organisations and the education by the adoptive parents, is taken into account.

An important principle, for instance, is that the European adoption organisations agree with the policy that adoption within the country of origin – domestic adoption – should be preferred above inter-country adoption. It is unfortunate, but irrefutable however, that in Third World countries domestic adoption is not sufficiently popular to be able to place all adoptable children in their country of birth. Domestic adoptions are, however, slowly growing in number in a few countries, such as India. Where European couples do adopt foreign, trans-racial babies, the adoptive parents are very concerned to take the roots of their adoptee very seriously. What you see today is that groups of adoptive parents travel to the country of origin of their child(ren) – the so-called 'roots journeys' – with the adolescent or young adult. These journeys are often organised by the adoption organisation.

The ethnicity of these trans-racial adoptive children is also dealt with in other ways. Reunions of adoptees of the same background, or even of the same Children's Home, are more and more frequently organised. Films with discussions about the importance of ethnicity, the reality of discrimination and the interaction between the adoption status and race difference are shown.

Without a doubt, we have to conclude that there is a large difference between countries in their thinking about trans-racial adoption. Can we understand this from history as well?

In Holland, phenomena like the 'one drop rule' (Lythcott-Haims 1994), the rule that maintains that a person is non-White if she/he has (at least) one drop of another race, are unknown – and there are a very large number of multi-racial people in Holland, people of partly Indonesian origin. Practising the 'one drop rule' seems to mean that the White part of the background in a person is completely ignored. The question could arise as to whether the Black part of multi-racial people is so strong and of such overwhelming importance. Has society any moral or ethical right to decide how a person has to feel about his ethnicity? Is there not a basic logic in the statement that the feeling of (multi)ethnicity is a very personal and intimate experience? A feeling that will be influenced by all ancestors of a person, by his life experiences and his personality set-up.

In most European countries there is no interference from authorities or powerful organisations with regard to inter-racial adoptions. In the United States, however, the National Association of Black Social Workers (NABSW) took a public stand in 1972 against trans-racial adoption (Lythcott-Haims 1994). The NABSW advocated placing Black children only in Black families. According to the NABSW, same-race placement is the only way for Black children to learn the survival techniques necessary to exist in a racist society. Therefore, placing Black children in foster-care or leaving them in a Children's Home should be preferred to placing them in White families. The effect has been that thousands of adoptable Black children (and the 'one drop rule' was used) never saw a family, or they were adopted by a Black family after spending extra years in a Children's Home.

A comparable development was seen in Great Britain in the last decade (Dale 1987). It more or less started with the statement by Black observers that, during the 1970s and earlier, potentially suitable Black families were disregarded as prospective adopters. These families failed to correspond to the White stereotype of an acceptable family (Hall 1986). However, until the beginning of the 1980s, there was no evidence of any real attempt to challenge the status quo. Trans-racial adoption was still the norm. In 1978, the influential organisation, British Agencies for Adoption and Fostering (BAAF), started a follow-up study of adoption families which had trans-racially adopted children aged between 12 and 14 years. The result of this study was controversial. On the one hand, it was found that most of the children (about 50) appeared to enjoy family life, they had good contact with their adoptive parents and siblings, and were doing well at school. There was nothing wrong with their self-esteem (Hall 1986). But, on the other hand, there was no sign that these children had developed a sense of racial identity. The picture was that these children had little knowledge or understanding of their racial origin and little contact with the culture of their origin. 'However', the researchers said, 'we must be realistic. Now and for some time to come, unless some Black children are to remain indefinitely in public care and be denied the benefits of any kind of family, some trans-racial placements will need to be made. It is hoped that in arranging such placements, proper attention will be paid to the willingness and capacity of the families to enable the Black child to establish and maintain contact with the Black community and develop a real sense of his own racial identity and heritage' (Hall 1986, p.70).

Partly due to this, BAAF tried harder to recruit Black families to care for Black children in public care. The intention was to ensure that trans-racial placements would become the rare exception rather than the general rule.

If we wish to understand the nature of the opposition to trans-racial adoption, we should not look at the needs of children. Dale (1987, p.9) concludes from his research that: 'Opposition arose neither from any observed failings of the practice nor from any lack of demand for it. The denial of white homes to black children rests on assumptions which have only a spurious link with the needs of individual children.'

The Children's Act of 1989 has legalised a policy of placing Black children only in Black families. Local Authorities are bound to consider culture, religion and ethnic needs when finding a home for a Black child. However, some adoption organisations – like Barnardos New Families in Yorkshire and Sandwell Social Services – have interpreted this 'bound to' as 'obliged to'. In Great Britain, the outcome has been that many Black children remain in public care or stay there years longer. For instance, 25 per cent of all children in care in a London Borough are of Asian origin.

How far some 'care takers' really do go was shown in the BBC2 programme *Taking Liberties* 23 May 1995. A 15-year-old girl of Asian origin stayed in care because the social worker at Sandwell Social Services had decided that she should be placed in an Asian family. The (Muslim) girl had told the social worker that she wanted to stay in a White family as an earlier placement in an Asian family had failed. It is not surprising, therefore, that considerable resistance to the official policy soon appeared from adoptive parents with a black foster child and representatives of some official organisations. Robin Sequeira, representative of the National Association of Directors of Social Services, has stated clearly that trans-racial adoption appears to be the only option available for many children in care. Robin has been largely responsible for the recently published report *Adoption: the future* by the Department of Health, Welsh Office, Home Office and Lord Chancellor's Department (1995). Some of the following conclusions in this report relate to the history of trans-racial adoption in Great Britain described above: 'Those assessing parents may have given culture and ethnicity an unjustifiably decisive influence and failed to make a balanced overall judgement of the parents' suitability'.

Also very clear is the following statement in the report: 'Considerations relating to a child's welfare should not be determined by principles which have their basis in dogma or political correctness. Such shackles tend to produce a narrow view about where the best wishes of a child lie'.

I think it is important to repeat here one of the conclusions of O'Brian, a Senior Lecturer of the Faculty of Humanities and Social Sciences in Hong Kong, and of Eurasian/Indian origin. He has done a cultural analysis of adoption in Hong Kong and tries to show why Chinese infants are placed with Caucasian families. He says:

> The movement against trans-racial adoption has its roots in the despair, anger, and pain that minority communities experience due to the structural racism that they have to endure in the Western countries in which they live. Nonetheless, in countries outside the West, trans-racial adoption offers for many children the only alternative to a life of prolonged impermanence with no sense of belonging. Professional workers have to take action and make plans that are in the best interests of the individual child concerned. This principle overrides all others. (O'Brian 1994, p.328).

It can be expected that, in Great Britain as well, the outcome will be that trans-racial adoption is back on the scene. The next step, however, should be that the adoption organisations in Great Britain will make use of the knowledge about trans-racial/inter-country adoption available in countries like Holland and Sweden. The relevant question is not so much whether trans-racial adoption has the right to exist, but how much more it should be done, the way in which the aspirant adoptive parents (and the older child) should be prepared for their adoption adventure and, later on, how they should be helped when, perhaps, intense problems arise in the family.

8.2 The influence of cultural differences

After having concluded in the former paragraph that trans-racial adoptions will grow in number, it is of great importance that these parents be guided as much as possible. An important question and a great worry for adoptive parents, with respect to trans-racial adoption, is to what extent their child will encounter discrimination, now or later on. Will adoptive children and, later on, adults be treated or approached differently from other people; differently from what they desire? Are these children more liable to find that doors remain closed when they apply for a job, or when they are looking for the right partner, or when they want to go and live somewhere? To put it yet another way, will prejudices play a major part in the subconscious, and sometimes quite conscious, judgements which occur in various situations?

It is difficult to deal with these questions extensively here. After all, in order to do this, a group of adoptive children will have to have become adults – quite apart from whether this problem will ever allow a conclusion. Societies are changeable and people's ideas and attitudes will change. People who belong to a certain group can remain invisible in a society for a relatively long time and not be discriminated against. Then, all of a sudden, they may enter a phase where they clearly do get discriminated against on various counts. But do adoptive children belong to a certain group? I will deal with this question first.

In sociological terms, a group is defined as a theoretical or psychological unit which consists of two or more people. These people experience this unit as a reality and in this they fulfil different roles, so as to create a certain social structure within the unit and often, also, a certain sub-culture. Groups which form a close unit show this by creating a clear sub-culture. One may think, for instance, of a group with a special interest, such as soccer fans, fellow believers or punk-rockers.

Will trans-racially adoptive children, when they have been with us for, say, twenty years, be regarded as South American or Indian and belonging to that particular ethnic group? For the moment I do not think so. In order to prove this supposition I will use several concepts from the brilliant work on the nature of prejudice by the American psychologist G.W. Allport (1954). He distinguishes racial and ethnic differences between people and groups. Racial differences arise from heredity factors. These are biological features which, in social interaction, can lead to various social interpretations. 'He is black so he will be...' According to Allport, it is not clear what should be regarded as racial differences. In order to find this out, an experiment is required in which children, who are as purely as possible from a different race, are placed in a different country with a different racial population immediately after birth. They grow up there and are then compared to the people of that particular country. When the groups in question are comparable on all points except race and yet show clear differences in behaviour, race can count as the reason for these differences. In fact, this is an experimental situation which applies to many adoptive children. That is why such a study is so important. However, is it possible to express any expectations about the results of such a study? I will make an attempt later on, but first I will discuss another way in which people and groups can be distinguished according to Allport: ethnic differences.

Ethnic differences came into being over the years. In particular, these are the differences between peoples which have been formed by their upbringing. The habits, attitudes, gestures, capacities (the language!) and ideas which have been passed on from one generation to the next. It is what makes a Frenchman a typical Frenchman, a Fleming typically Flemish and a Welshman a genuine Welshman. In connection with this, some psychologists speak of 'basic personality'. They believe that the distinctive characteristics in the personalities of members of an ethnic group arise from the upbringing.

Now the key question for us is: to what ethnic group do the adoptive children that come to us from various countries belong, or what ethnic group do they appear to belong to? I say 'appear' because, in a lot of cases, trans-racial adoptive children clearly look different from other English, Swedish, Dutch or Belgian people but behave in a completely European manner. With this statement, the first, and probably the most important, reason is given as to why I believe that, for adoptive children, the danger of discrimination in important areas of life will be small. After all, adoptive children arrive in the Netherlands, Belgium, France, Sweden, the USA and other countries at an early to very early age. They will learn to master the new language perfectly, including the local dialect. Also, subconsciously they will take over various (small) characteristics of being Belgian, Dutch, French or German – for instance, certain gestures, habits or a particular way of dressing. In short, a number of the adoptive children will only differ from other local children on one important point: their appearance. In all other respects they will be recognisable as fellow-countrymen. This means that possible discrimination cannot be based on cultural differences, for there aren't any. On the contrary, the child will be strikingly similar to other children. Why 'striking'? Because, subconsciously, we may expect small differences. It is very likely that many people will be surprised when a five-year-old Indian girl addresses them in Cockney English or the Frisian dialect. Then, the behaviour of the child does not fit certain (vague) expectations we have. Will not a short habituation-process be enough to reach adjustment of our expectations?

8.3 Is discrimination due to differences in appearance?

Now, is there a great chance of being discriminated against only because of the different appearance, the racial distinction of the adoptee? For the time being, I do not think this will be the case in countries where multi-cultural or multi-ethnic families are well accepted. In order to explain this, I will once more use several recent theoretical studies.

In the social sciences, a lot of research has been conducted into the relationship between the individual and the group to which he or she belongs. It can be said that every human being belongs to a number of groups. The group to which a person belongs differs depending on the stage of life that person has reached. The group memberships of a young child are different from those of an adult. The primary concerns of the child are the family and playmates in the neighbourhood and in school. As the child grows older, the number of groups to which he belongs will expand and the child will grow more conscious of differences between groups and of the groups to which he belongs. In sociological terms, the latter are called 'membership-groups'. These 'membership-groups' are of great importance for the formation of identity consciousness. 'Identity consciousness' means that someone can be identified as one and the same person by himself and other people with respect to the way he thinks and acts in different situations and at different moments. He always remains the same person.

Only gradually does a person secure an identity in his or her life. During the childhood years this process passes relatively unnoticed. But, from the on-set of puberty, identity problems tend to occur. In this period, feelings of safety and security, which are closely related to a stable identity-consciousness, are liable to suffer tremendously. The great physical changes related to puberty form an important cause of possible identity problems. After all, the adolescent has a lot to learn. He has to accept himself, his physical appearance and things which he is or is not good at. At the same time, he or she is constantly reminded of his or her role as a future man or woman and he or she will have to accept his or her sexual identity. Therefore, the period of puberty is often a period of reviewing and reorientation of the personality. For many youngsters it is a difficult phase on the road to adulthood.

Does this phase involve special problems for adoptive children? Will they, especially in this period, wonder whether they are different? These are essential, existentially-oriented questions which are not easy to answer. From the follow-up research among the Thai children, we can conclude that adoptive children do have more trouble accepting certain external characteristics. For instance, some think they are too short compared to the tall Europeans. Others experience that they are indeed different for the first time in their lives. Often this is a reason to start pondering over the past, their country of origin and their birth parents. As a consequence, there may be the danger of feeling torn between two loyalties: those of their ethnic and racial past with their birth parents and the compelling tangibility of being raised as a European by European parents. Will they, perhaps, as some adoptive parents fear, want to consciously orientate themselves to their heritage and belong to this other people? In other words, will they have a desire to belong to another group (reference group) and do they aspire to this?

The possibility of the latter happening does not seem very likely. A person who was raised in a particular country from his earliest childhood will indeed experience these ties as compelling. This will certainly be the case when these ties and group memberships satisfy this person in his most essential needs – such as safety and security. Obviously this means that the age of the child when placed in the family is of importance to the way in which the loyalty problem takes shape. The older the child is when placed in the family, the stronger the memories will be of the country of origin and the habits and customs there – in short, his ethnic background. A child of, for instance, six years of age will have experienced a considerable cultural formation already. Will this child still be capable of developing a different identity in a satisfying manner? Or will the above-mentioned loyalty problem always play an interfering role with these children in particular? Apart from this, the question, which cannot be answered here, remains as to whether it is at all possible for a person entering a new family to gain a satisfying identity, when elsewhere, up to a certain age, his most essential needs were not satisfied. When this question is answered with 'no', it is most likely that this person will not feel at home anywhere. He does not possess any obvious group memberships, nor does he have a stable ethnic identity. These are the people who really remain in-between. What this in-betweenness conveys is strongly focused towards a feeling of not being at home anywhere, of being a nobody, to put it very negatively. The story of Peter in the previous chapter is a clear example of this feeling of being in-between.

Will the outside world, in a subtle manner, still force the adoptive child, which does look different, into this other role? They might give the adoptive child the feeling that it does indeed belong to a different group. In my opinion, the mere difference in outward appearance is not enough reason for this. Even when this person, as discussed above, temporarily focuses on his past, this should not have any consequences for various kinds of external behaviour. I should add one important point to this. As adults, adoptive children will never form a clearly distinct minority as, for instance, immigrant workers do. Many forms of discrimination are directed towards people who clearly belong to a certain group and present themselves as such. Nevertheless, there is the question as to whether the creation of a minority is the result of discrimination or whether a process of discrimination is initiated due to voluntary isolation. I will let this 'chicken or egg' discussion rest.

I do, however, want to make a very specific point. Since the mid-1980s, the phenomenon of foreign adoption has been in the news regularly and, often, in a negative manner. Stories about illegal adoptions from certain countries alternate with lamentations by parents whose adoption seems to have failed. They pour out their hearts on television, on the radio and in the newspapers. Let me, however, make this remark right away: quite apart from what I will say next, from my own practice I know how difficult it can be in some families for years on end – even with parents who love to devote themselves completely to their child and who do not have important problems with any other children in their family. Nevertheless, these parents can, probably unintentionally, stimulate the stigmatisation of trans-racial adoptive children by giving a certain meaning to the negative publicity. They literally start showing the identifying mark: he is a trans-racial adoptive child so he will be... More and more adoptive children will become adults in the final decade of this century. They will become increasingly better informed about what is generally said about them and how they are judged. Thus we see that these adults are letting themselves be heard in the year 1995. They are forced into a situation where they have to defend themselves and there is even some group formation going on already. As long as these groups of foreign adoptive children can focus together on personal interests and mutual contacts, I do not worry about this. On the contrary, I support these initiatives wholeheartedly but I would greatly regret an element of self-defence also sneaking into this group formation.

Returning to the question of whether I think the chance of discrimination of racially different foreign adoptive children is great, I would answer that with a 'no', for the time being. I think that only a few adoptive children will, in their youth and/or adult life, experience some sort of serious discrimination in important areas. The principal arguments for this are:

○ The adoptive child will grow up completely as a fellow-countryman and mainly focus himself on the society in question in his thoughts and actions.

○ I do not think the chance of such a group formation that results in a distinct minority group (for instance, adoptive Colombians) with its own structure and culture is very great, unless negative stimuli from the social environment (for example, local authorities, press, organisations of social service) give rise to this.

So, when we view the situation from the perspective of the adoptive child, I think there is little cause for discrimination. The only thing remaining then is the different outward appearance, which may perhaps evoke associations with certain minority groups and therefore give rise to discrimination. In the next section I will discuss this problem in further detail.

8.4 Data from research

Obviously, attempts have been made to gain more practical information about preventing forms of discriminating behaviour with regard to adoptive children. This was done by enquiring after the extent and nature of the contact that adoptive children have with peers and the nature of the reactions of adults in the direct social environment.

The first question that was asked was to what extent parents think their adoptive child has more, equally much or less contact with other children in comparison to peers. On the whole, adoptive children do not differ from other children in this. When a distinction is made with respect to the country of origin, it appears that European children all have nearly equal amount of contact with their peers whereas Asian children tend to have more contacts with other children.

For the time being, I will gather from this that the children, no matter where they are from, can get along fairly well with other children. Children accept each other but they can also be very harsh, at least in the eyes of the adult. In the perception of the child, this harshness may be nothing more than teasing.

Obviously, to us an important question is whether the child is sometimes teased with respect to its being 'different', and how the child and the parents respond to this. From the group of children who regularly hang out with other children, 25 per cent appear to be bullied about being 'different'. This mainly concerns older children. With toddlers this hardly ever occurs, according to the parents. This agrees with the results from other studies. It appears that children up to four or five years of age do not pick their playmates on grounds of racial differences. These differences only become important with time. Most children are not bothered about the teasing. With respect to teasing about being different, the complexion, as such, does not seem to be a major factor; other features are more important. Indian children are teased a lot less than other Asian and even Greek children. Perhaps Indian children come close to some kind of Western 'ideal beauty' and perhaps this is less so with Eastern-Asian children.

Now, what is the nature of these types of teasing? From the remarks made by parents with respect to this, it generally seems that clearly noticeable physical characteristics give rise to all sorts of comments and terms of abuse. The following four characteristics are especially subject to abuse: slant of the eyes, a flat nose, skin colour and, in some cases, body height. The child is sometimes teased with the fact that his parents are not the biological parents. An anthology of the terms of abuse include: chink, gook, nigger, paki and tiny. We can conclude from this that it is no different from ordinary children's practice and can be compared with terms of abuse such as redhead, four-eyes and beanpole, but this abuse can hurt children considerably. Unfortunately, this kind of behaviour among children cannot be prevented completely. After all, people express their aggression in different ways and children often do so by name-calling. On the other hand, it usually only means a short communication breakdown between the children and a little later they can all play quite happily with each other again.

3.5 Several warnings
Although I have been rather optimistic about the chances of any negative discrimination in the above, I certainly wish to add a word of warning for parents. It can and does happen that a child is teased considerably with its outward appearance or even constantly harrassed, sometimes by the same classmates. In our clinical practice, we have come across this several times and we have learned that this makes a tremendous impression on the child. We see such negative behaviour from classmates occurring from the age of eleven or twelve. After all, from that age onwards physical appearance becomes an important factor for youngsters. They start looking at each other more and more and judging each

other physically. Striking features have a tendency to attract a lot of attention. Trans-racial adoptive children can have striking features; the girls because of early puberty, the boys by clearly growing less tall than average – all this, both in girls and in boys, apart from specific racial characteristics.

However, not all children or adolescents will tell their parents what kind of problems they have at school. The youngsters may have serious problems with the way they are treated in the neighbourhood and/or at school but they may hardly, or not at all, want to talk to their parents about it. Sometimes they are ashamed of being so concerned about the teasing, or there is very little they tell their parents during this particular stage of life anyway. In any case, adoptive parents would always do well to be very watchful for any problems their child may have with its physical appearance. Teasing remarks from other children can pretty much spoil any fun the child may have at school. How can you know whether there is something wrong in school when a child only tells you very little? Often it is indicated by the following striking changes in behaviour:

- Suddenly the child starts to dislike going to school and day-by-day hesitates longer before going to school, but in the end usually does go.
- The child becomes more quiet, as if bothered by something.
- The child brings up subjects that have something to do with teasing, albeit indirectly. For example, the child asks the parents certain things about their school days.
- Generally the child seeks attention and support from the parents or one particular friend or classmate more often than before.

What is the best way for parents to respond when they notice that their child is frequently teased because of his different looks? First, all parents should make their child aware of the fact that he is different as far as appearance is concerned, that he belongs to a different race. And that this is certainly not a reason to feel inferior or different, but that he should reckon with various forms of discrimination, including teasing from peers. This education by the parents, which has to be given at a very young age, will prevent that 'being different' suddenly being experienced as a terrible shock. It can also help if the parents show the child the cultural contribution and heritage of his country of origin. It would be very helpful to have some books and literature at home and watch television programmes about the country of origin or about adoption in general. Nick Banks, a chartered clinical psychologist specialising in work with Black children and families, gives in his *Techniques for direct identity work with Black children* quite a number of very practical suggestions to adoptive parents of a Black child (Banks 1992).

In spite of this, the child will still be teased sometimes. The child should know that if he cannot deal with it himself by, for example, treating the teasing child in the same manner as he treats him, the parents and the teachers are always there for him (with advice). Hopefully, this latter point will prevent two important effects:

- Teasing behaviour of classmates and children in the neighbourhood will go on for years, without them knowing what they are doing to the discriminated child.

- The victim bottles-up his negative emotions. The psychological consequences can be very serious. The child may, for example, develop strong feelings of inferiority or feelings of hatred towards White fellow-countrymen – may arise almost unawares. This makes it more difficult for the person in question to acquire a stable and satisfying identity.

To conclude, several points of interest. Discriminating behaviour by youngsters amongst themselves is usually related to other behaviour – meaning that when an adoptive child complains about being teased, one should investigate why there is teasing going on. One should not assume straight away that other people are entirely to blame. Sometimes it is the behaviour of the adoptive child himself which contributes strongly to this kind of behaviour. If this behaviour changes, the classmates will change as well. In short, with respect to discrimination, one should look at the interaction between the youngsters, not just to one side.

Adults, unlike children, are sometimes inclined to exercise a certain positive form of discrimination whilst the adoptive child is still very young. Some adoptive parents indicate that people in the neighbourhood all react in an extremely positive manner and that no one seems to be unkind. Often people's reactions are 'what a cute little kid', 'how brave of you', or comments to that effect, and give the child unhealthy amounts of sweets. Obviously, adoptive parents do not really need this kind of behaviour. If the child has just been placed in the family it may even lead to enormous problems, as I have tried to make clear in Chapter 6, but this will probably remain one of the inevitable side effects of foreign and trans-racial adoption, along with the sometimes annoying behaviour of other children. Anyway, let the reader be warned: better safe than sorry.

Just how the adoptive child himself will cope with his origin while in the process of developing his own identity will have to remain uncertain, for the time being. The phenomenon of foreign and trans-racial adoption is too new for this question to be answered. Hopefully, an answer will soon be given to the question of the extent to which the feeling of being 'different' helps or, conversely, delays the development of a personal identity.

Finally, what can we conclude with respect to the question of whether adoptive children are discriminated against, as was asked at the beginning of this section? Obviously, it is certainly true for some of the children that they are teased and treated in a negative manner due to their outward appearance. However, to what extent this will lead to deliberate discrimination later on is hard to predict. Nevertheless, for several children, and adults, this can be expected in certain situations – including economic developments (unemployment) and experiences with foreigners (for instance, looking for a place to live in certain districts of big cities and looking for a job with certain companies).

Of great importance to adoptive children is whether or not their parents have prepared them well enough to be able to cope with certain forms of teasing. Obviously, being teased about physical appearance should not lead to feelings of inferiority. Parents should talk about these matters with their children. Parents in our study, who had stated that they had done so elaborately, declared that the child showed very little concern for teasing after that. Besides, this interest in physical appearance is typically something which becomes important during puberty. Then it will become clear whether or not the adoptive child accepts its 'different' appearance. This will be determined, to an important extent, by the preceding phase of the upbringing.

To conclude, I leave you with the comment that, in my opinion, the possible negative side effect of discrimination because of racial characteristics can never compensate for the completely hopeless situation which most of our adoptive children leave behind: a situation in which there is also discrimination of for instance, children of single mothers, children of mixed races or children with parents suffering from leprosy. Sometimes this discrimination is so complete that it threatens the bare existence, let alone there being sufficient opportunity for individual and social development. Nevertheless, the fear of discrimination exists with many people and some couples decline to adopt for this reason. For the same reason, other couples state a preference for a certain race, and – it should not be left unsaid – this rarely concerns Negroid children.

CHAPTER 9

The Adoption Status Should be Discussable for the Parents as Well as for the Children

9.1 Psychological parenthood

The child has arrived, the first difficult or perhaps easy months have passed. Hopefully, the process of mutual adaptation and the formation of a close parent–child bond have started. Psychological parenthood will develop, slowly but surely. Is this at all possible, many may wonder. Are adoptive parents or non-genetic parents indeed fully capable of replacing the biological parents? Is it not the case that biological parenthood is a prerequisite for psychological parenthood? I, and many others with me, would answer this question in the negative. Whether an adult becomes the psychological parent of a child depends on the amount of time, and the quality of the time, this adult spends with the child. The day-to-day experiences, hanging out together, sharing good times and bad times, guiding the growth and development of the child are what matters here. Obviously, biological parenthood is a fundamental human fact. However, the mere biological aspect is insufficient to equate it with the complex notion of parenthood. Therefore, it has justly been noted – opposing the previous statement – that adoption is possible only by virtue of the psychological parenthood being not merely a matter of blood relationship but something developing in everyday life which parent and child share with each other.

This means that after the child is born one cannot immediately speak of psychological parenthood. At the very most, one may expect that this has started to grow during pregnancy and after birth. It grows stronger as time goes by and the bonds between parents and child become increasingly tighter and, following naturally from this, a possible separation by death or other reasons will be experienced as more and more painful as the child grows up – quite apart from the negative consequences which sudden separations have for children in a particular developmental phase.

These negative effects are always – very justly – put forward by organisations in this field in order to advocate that adoption should take place at the earliest possible age, for the child as well as for the adoptive parents. Psychological parenthood will develop better when the child is placed in the adoptive family at the earliest possible age. There are two obvious parties that come into play in all this: on the one hand, the parents – who both differ with respect to the way in which psychological parenthood will form itself – and, on the other hand, the child – who will respond to the parents in a manner depending on the age at which, and the condition in which, he enters the family. The processes which will eventually lead to a strong mutual bond do not necessarily have the same effect on both parties. The child may feel a strong bond with his new parents before they do. For the child this is necessary in order to get the feelings of safety and security which are of such vital importance to him.

The position is different for adults. For them, the sense of responsibility will (have to) play an important role. They realise that they are responsible for the adoptive child, now and in the future, but, for them, the response of the child to the parental care will also be of importance. Emotional ties do not spring from responsibility alone. Again, the day-to-day experiences determine this. Just how decisive these experiences are, and how long it can take for adults to get the feeling that the child does indeed belong to them, will be illustrated by the following example:

Sujong

Sujong is the third child of a family which already has two adoptive children. He arrived with an estimated age of three years and with the developmental age of a one-year-old. He was seriously undernourished and could hardly walk due to his swollen belly and lack of strength. His medical report stated that Sujong did have some impairment but, apart from this, he would be a healthy and cheerful child.

The first few days went by without notable difficulties for the parents, but then it all started. According to the parents, two patterns alternated: 'Physical and psychological withdrawal and long periods of rocking and overall apathy' and 'crying and screaming for hours on end, usually without an obvious reason'. Towards strangers, however, the child was quite normal and friendly. Furthermore, the parents described how negative their experiences of these first months of adjustment were. They did not receive a lot of support from other parents and acquaintances. When they saw the child, there was not any particular reaction. The child evoked feelings of pity with these people; after all, he looked so unhealthy and pitiful. After six months of conflict, agitation, insomnia and problems with the child, and uncertainty and despair on their part, they decided to consult an Educational Bureau.

The psychologist began by making it clear that she could well imagine that the entire situation was becoming too much for the parents. This turned out to hit the mark because at last there was someone who did not immediately assume that the parents ought to lavish love on the child or that the problems were probably not so bad and would soon blow over. She also brought the parents into contact with other adoptive parents. In the following six months few notable changes took place in the child's behaviour, although he did sleep more peacefully. His health improved considerably. His belly started to subside and his arms and legs grew more firm. He was also able to walk, and seemed happier.

The fact that the parents could at least talk to other people about their problems, somewhat eased the strain for them. They were able to be more objective and then very slowly start to accept the child and see his positive qualities.

Approximately one and a half to two years after his arrival in the family, his parents state that there is improvement. Sujong no longer responds in an extreme manner when he does not get his way. The apathetic behaviour has even disappeared completely. The contact with the other two children, of which the youngest is five, is improving too. Sometimes they even play together a little.

He does, however, clearly try his parents. When his father comes home at night he usually sits with him and tries to get him to do all sorts of things. This particularly happens when he just has had an argument with his mother. The first few times his father really fell for it. But now he is in the habit of first asking his wife how Sujong is, as soon as he gets home. Looking back, both parents state that during the first couple of years they often felt they were unable to cope and that Sujong and they just didn't hit it off. Since there had hardly been any problems with their first two adoptive children, this was entirely new to them. Several times they even contemplated having Sujong placed in a different family. However, that same psychologist deterred them from doing so. She pointed out the consequences of the large developmental impairment, the neglect as experienced by Sujong and the great shock of the enormous changes for a child who cannot yet understand anything of all this. She emphasised that they had to be patient and, particularly, not react in an extreme manner to Sujong's peculiar behaviour. He would take years to make a reasonable recovery. Thanks to the patience and practical directions of the psychologist, the stamina of both parents and the slow improvements in Sujong's behaviour, they came through this difficult first stage.

Although this example may seem rather extreme, we know from experience that psychological parenthood does not always come about without pain and effort. We know that it can take a long time before parents get the feeling that the child is actually part of the family and that it is inextricably bound to the family. With respect to this, one should think in terms of months or several years rather than in weeks. Parents may have to go through a lot of hardship, especially with the arrival of older children. Finally, there is one important point I would like to emphasise with regard to the example of Sujong: the benefit these parents gained from being able to talk with others about the problems at a relatively early stage. In this case, this openness turned out to be the first step towards solving the problems.

9.2 Openness about adoptive parenthood has many advantages

With the Sujong example there is a certain openness as far as the problems in the family are concerned. I would like to expand the necessity for this openness to more aspects related to adoption. All adoptive parents have to deal with the fundamental fact that their child has different biological parents and a different biological family. From various studies and clinical experiences (Lifton 1983), we know that many adoptive children confront their parents with this fact. In several Western countries this has led to considerably more openness amongst the adoptive parents concerning the adoption status and everything that goes with it. Unfortunately, in non-Western countries there is not yet such openness. There, children are given up frequently but there is very little interest in adopting children. Also, in Western countries, it is debated whether adoptive parenthood is essentially different from biological parenthood and whether or not this difference should be expressed in the upbringing of the children. Summing up, there are two views: those who emphasise that adoptive parenthood does not or only slightly differs from biological parenthood and those who believe that it does.

However, the adoptive parents from the former group do admit that the start of life with the adoptive child is different. They also realise the difference between them and other parents as far as receiving the child is concerned. Nevertheless, they believe that the extensive period of growing and living together reduces these differences to a minimum. Some even go so far as to claim that they do not note any differences in their parenthood, that the adoptive child is their own child, so to speak, and that the child himself does not attach great interest to the adoption status, but noted that the wish is often father to the thought. Often these parents feel no need to have contact with other adoptive parents and withdraw from everything that has anything to do with adoption. Their opinion can be influenced by several factors; they may have received the child at a very early age and perhaps it hardly differs from them racially. For the child himself, the adoption status is not self-evident and something he has learnt to live with, whereas this is not always the case for inter-racial and/or older adoptive children.

The other group of adoptive parents are very aware of the adoption status of their child right from the start. The matter is discussed frequently and, when the child is from a different country, plans are made to visit that country. Some parents go so far as to try and learn the language of the country (Spanish, Korean, Chinese), even when the child has long lost command of that language or perhaps never had any. Generally, these parents maintain regular contact with other adoptive parents and are well informed about important adoptive matters. On their bookshelf we find many books dealing with the country of origin and adoption. Kirk (1981) has indicated these ideas by means of the dichotomy, Rejection-of-Difference and Acknowledgement-of-Difference (R.D.-attitude and A.D.-attitude). With respect to the R.D.-attitude, he states that 'the adoptive experience was essentially not different from that of the mainstream family', while in the other case 'real differences were recognised'. Subsequently, a clear relation was found in the Kirk study and in the research conducted by the Adoption Centre (the Thai-research) between the attitude towards adoptive parenthood and the relationship with the child. An open attitude has a positive effect on this relationship.

There is a second type of openness of adoptive parents which is of interest to the relationship with their child. In order to explain this, I will come back to what I described in Chapter 2 as the 'internal and external orientation of parents'.

The majority of adoptive parents consist of the more internally-oriented parents. They are the people who love to raise children and who see the responsibility of the upbringing as an important fulfilment of their lives. Usually, these are parents who are involuntarily childless in a primary or secondary sense (the desired second or third child does not come). Approximately 90 per cent of all adoptive parents belong to this group.

A second group of adoptive parents has rather abstract motives for adoption. They say they want to contribute to the fight against global overpopulation by limiting the number of children of their own. They may also be greatly moved by the hardship of many children in the Third World; they want to help a child in need. These couples are more externally oriented. When making this distinction, we should bear in mind that this is not a matter of either/or. Both groups of couples like to bring up children. And I repeat, this should be the principal reason for all couples to adopt.

However, sometimes there are important gradual differences in the motivation for admitting a child into the family. An extreme internal or external orientation may have a negative effect on the upbringing. Expectations can become too high, which may cause difficulties. The child is not seen as an independent person with his own problems, possibilities and wishes. The child may have too much of an abstract function, for example to terminate a process of mourning caused by involuntary childlessness, a stillborn child or a child who died at a later age, or to fulfil feelings of global idealism and altruism.

We advise all applicant adoptive parents to have a critical and, therefore, open attitude toward their motives for adopting a (foreign) child and the emotions and expectations related to this. They should ask themselves whether they are prepared to make important changes in certain views, behaviour and ways of upbringing. This is an absolute prerequisite for the successful development of a child with his own unique personality and often difficult history.

To sum up, I would advise all adoptive parents to acknowledge the uniqueness of their parenthood, to themselves as well as to people around them. But it is of the greatest importance to do so towards the child. They would also do well to critically contemplate their motives for adoption, mostly in order to prevent negative influences on the upbringing of the child caused by certain adoptive motives.

9.3 Openness with respect to the subject of adoption

The subtle and sensitive process of mutual adjustment and the development of psychological parenthood works out differently in every family. This is logical and obvious, for children are different, and so are the conditions in which they are adopted – their age and physical condition on arrival in the family, the parents, and so on and so forth.

However, there is one question which all parents will have to deal with. How and when do I talk to my child about his 'adoption status'? A great many books and journals pay attention to this issue: the right of the child to be informed about his adoption status and the parents obligation to do so. In the Netherlands and Belgium – although there is no legal stipulation – and in other countries, this obligation has been emphatically established. At the application for adoption, if the child is twelve years or older (this used to be 14 years old), the Judge has to ask the child his opinion concerning the adoption.

Obviously, it is of even greater importance that children who were adopted at an early age know just how they came to their parents, from the earliest stage in life in which they are able to understand this. For most parents, nowadays, this goes without saying. This is due to the completely different situation which marks present foreign adoption. To these parents, the fact of adoption is an entirely obvious event which can be dealt with in an open manner. Secrecy is no longer an issue, supposing it were at all possible to begin with. All experts agree that it is extremely harmful if the child is informed by, for instance, an arbitrary member of the family or children at school rather than his parents. The suffering which is inflicted upon a person in this way is described by Sophocles (Ramondt 1984) in the Greek tragedy *Oedipus*:

> This I (Oedipus) do not want to keep from you, now that I am a victim of such fear. Who would I rather tell than you (Iokaste, wife and mother of Oedipus) now that I have to wade through a pool of suffering? My father descended from Korinthos, Polubos, my mother's name was Merope, a Dorian. I was considered the greatest among the people, until a fate came over me – worth astonishment, however not serious consideration – for at a banquet a man, who was utterly drunk on wine, said that I was a young cuckoo in the nest which sheltered me. I kept my anger to myself that day, albeit with great difficulty, but early the following day I went to my father and mother for an explanation. They addressed their wrath to the man who had let this slip. Their attitude gave me joy; nevertheless, the expression kept torturing me, ate deep into my heart. (p.169)

Then, most confused, Oedipus leaves his parental home to ask the oracle of Delphi for advice. There he learns what a terrible fate is bestowed upon him (he will murder his father, marry his mother and eventually die in exile). The theme of Oedipus' insecurity with respect to his origin continuously speaks through Sophocles' entire story.

It is interesting to see how Sophocles shows in this tragedy just how important it is for Oedipus to know what is going to happen to him, even though it is predicted that this knowledge will be his downfall. Although this story has extreme sides, the most important elements regarding status information are incorporated into it. These are: the way parents inform the child, the child's response to this, the extent to which the child is aware of his adoption status and experiences this as 'being different', whether the child thinks about his origin and, finally, the interaction with peers in relation to this 'being different'. Generally, 'telling' is considered something which both parents should do. Only in a few families is this done by the mother alone. Sometimes the other children – if any – are involved in the conversation.

Of the group of adoptive parents that was examined first, 75 per cent of the parents who have already started informing the child turn out to have done so deliberately. With a limited number of families the subject came up accidentally. The parents were also asked whether they were reluctant to have the conversation and whether they thought the conversation as such to be difficult. The fact that 96 per cent state not to have been reluctant to do it at all is a very positive result. I see this result as confirmation of the aforementioned assumption that the entire issue of status information is a completely obvious matter to virtually all adoptive parents with a foreign adoptive child. Therefore, it is not surprising that in our Thai research, in which all children were five and a half years old or older, all parents had discussed the subject of adoption with their child.

For the time being, the conclusion that the information issue is considered hardly problematic seems correct. This result may be of support to the limited group of parents for whom the status information is a delicate issue. It remains a fact that eventually all parents have to talk with their child about his status themselves. It is absolutely unacceptable if this did not happen, even if only by a few couples.

A following question is: at what age do parents discuss the subject of adoption with the child for the first time? With respect to this, the experts seem to agree less than about the necessity for information as described above. The discussion now focuses on whether the information should start at the age of, for instance, two years or should one wait until the child is able to understand things better, say at an age of five or six years.

Those who support the idea that the child should be as young as possible state that the child can get used to certain sounds at an early age, and that early information is easier for the parents as well. Those who support the second view claim that certain risks are involved when confronting a child with delicate life problems at too early an age, and that a very young child will not understand any of it anyway. Before one begins with status information, the child should have a sufficient sense of reality and should be able to understand what it is about. This requires some insight into family relations, the aspect of having children and the existence of other people. According to this view, it is not wise to talk to children about adoption before they are four years old.

However, it seems that most parents begin to inform their child about his status around his fourth birthday. Some adoptive parents start the education at a very early age. I do, however, have to say that I consider it unrealistic to consciously start status information with one- or two-year-olds. I believe the effects of this are questionable. The results from the research do indeed confirm this, for it appeared from the comments by the parents in our group that 80 per cent of the children younger than four years did not understand any of it. By the way, Femmie Juffer has published a most attractive book in this context. In her book *I am Shira* she demonstrates, by means of drawings and stories of a six-year-old girl, how one can talk about adoption with children between the ages of four and about eight.

The clinical practice provides data in which serious behavioural problems or even psychoses occurring at a later age are related to talking about adoption at too early an age. I presume that there are great risks in the combination of a very sensitive and insecure child and parents who talk about procreation and adoption with great emphasis, and in a way which is not sufficiently adjusted to the age of the child (especially with two- or three-year-olds). The child senses that something important is being told by the way the parents are acting. He does not yet understand a thing of what is being said, but the subject as a whole – family formation, the arrival with father and mother – may even come across as threatening (in exceptional cases, that is).

In general, I believe that the information can be started at the age of about four, but gradually and adjusted to the level of comprehension of the adoptive child. The most ideal situation is when the entire matter of adoption is treated as a completely natural family situation by all members of the family. That way the adoptee may experience that it was never deliberately talked about at a particular moment: he knew all along that he had entered the family in a special way and the subject was often joked about. A nice example of how the matter might be discussed can be found in the journal *2+* by the Dutch Association for Foster Families:

My story: by Ernst and Mummy.

Far away, across the sea, there is a country called Lebanon.

In that country there was a little boy, he did not have a daddy or a mummy to look after him.

Jan and Emmy lived in Holland.

Jan and Emmy said: We would like to look after that little child.

Jan made a closet and a cradle.

They put the little clothes in a big suitcase, then they went on the plane, to Lebanon.

Jan and Emmy liked the little child very much. They called him: Ernst.

The little child grew bigger. He learned how to walk and how to speak.

He called Jan: daddy.

He called Emmy: mummy.

Now Ernst is six years old. There are many things he can do: ride a bike, carpentry, sing and draw.

He even has a sister, all curly-haired, her name is Klaartje.

Note that this story lacks the difficulty of the reality of another mum and dad. Especially for older children, who can have a clear memory of their biological parents (usually only the mother), this may continue to play an important role in the entire perception of being adopted. As I said before, adoptive parents should not only talk about the biological parents as realistically as possible but also in the most positive way possible. A special problem is which term of address should be given to the biological parents. In her very clearly written book about how you can talk about the biological parents with your adoptive child, Betty Heeg (1991) of the Dutch adoption organisation *Stichting Kind en Toekomst* (Association of Child and Future) opted for the term 'the other mummy'. On the whole, it may seem slightly cold and insensitive to speak in terms of 'the woman from whom you were born' or a variation of this. Talking about the first mother should be done in positive terms, but, the child must not get the idea that she is still waiting for him. Such information is an unnecessary strain on the child, which is on the whole undesirable. Other, frequently used terms of address are: your first mother, your birthmother, your natural mother. But not, for instance, 'real mother', for if all is well the adoptive parent – the one who has created a genuine parent–child relationship – will consider himself the real parent.

Finally, the parents were asked whether the attitude of the child had changed after the parents had talked about adoption. Again it appears that adoptive parents hardly have to worry about the aspect of status information. Only a few parents mention a changed attitude of the child, and then mostly in a positive sense. A greater affection has developed after the talk. This result agrees completely with what was discussed above. Being open about the adoption status has a positive effect on family relations and increases the faith the adoptee has in his parents.

9.4 I am adopted

Jaffee and Fanshel (1970) found that it is only between their sixth and ninth life-year that children grow aware of their adoption status. All I can do is confirm this. Of the overall majority of the children that are four years old or less, the parents claim that they are not clearly aware of their adoption status. From five years onwards, however, the overall majority are aware of their adoption status. Obviously we should consider here that this 'becoming aware' is a process.

Children do not become aware overnight of something as complicated as adoption. This occurs gradually and is certainly not always immediately visible to the parents. If parents say that at a certain age children realise that they are adopted, this does not exclude the possibility that, before that, all sorts of related thoughts were formed in their little minds. I say this because it must not be gathered from this data that status information should start at a later age, for instance, at six. A general rule is that, for a gradual introduction, the age for kindergarten is most obvious and also gives the best guarantee that the parents will be the first ones to tell the child about it.

It was also asked how the children feel about being adopted. Only a few children, all over twelve years old, are really having problems coping with it. The overall majority are comfortable with it. With respect to this it should be noted that particularly older children, especially during puberty, from their twelfth birthday, are considered to start thinking of their adoption as problematic. Indeed, this appeared to be the case with the follow-up of the Thai research. During that particular stage of life, parents are advised to pay renewed attention to the subject. For instance, it may be beneficial to find out what the child thinks of his birth parents. Apart from that, the adoptee should be given copies of the adoption documents. It is often sensible to give these to the child when he or she is about twelve years old. Remember that the child's past is, as it were, the property of the child. Dealing with this openly, no matter how difficult you may secretly find this as an adoptive father/mother, has only positive effects on the mutual relationship. I have called this the second adoption paradox. Bringing the background and the birth parents close to the child enhances the relationship between the adoptive parents and the child. Keeping them away, approaching them in a negative manner or denying them causes a certain alienation between the adoptive parents and the child and may, perhaps, even enhance that which the parents are so afraid of: a child who is continuously pre-occupied with his background and wants to go and look for his birth parents at a very early age.

Sometimes, however, children in this developmental phase do not yet want to talk about their background at all. They are much too busy growing up. But this can also be a very deeply-imbedded identity problem which they particularly do not want to discuss with their adoptive parents. For the time being they deny wanting to go to their country of origin. The reasons for this may lie in a fear of confrontation with the birth parent(s). The child does not have the slightest idea how to deal with this or which attitude to adopt towards his adoptive parents. The child does not yet want to have to deal with these complicated issues. In 1973, John Triseliotis conducted an interesting and widely-used study with respect to the need of adoptees to know more about their background. For nearly all 68 adoptees who were questioned by him, one question in particular turned out to be important: 'Why did my parents put me up for adoption?' They especially wanted to know whether or not they had been planned by their birth parents. To illustrate this I quote an example of the reaction of a grown woman, as given by Triseliotis (1973):

> If ever I had a baby out of wedlock I wouldn't have it adopted. My children mean a tremendous lot to me. Either my mother or my father must have had such feelings for me...then why give me up? Was there something wrong with me or with them? I have this obsession about being adopted and my mother is the only one who can help me to understand. (pp.111–112)

This woman projected her own motherly emotions onto her mother and thus reached the, for her, amazing question of why her mother had given her up. She herself would never take such a step, since her children mean a tremendous lot to her.

For the self-image of adopted persons it may, perhaps, be of some importance to have some fairly detailed information concerning the past at their disposal. Since, in many cases concerning non-European adoption, there is no information whatsoever about the biological parents, a certain image will have to be created by the adoptive parents. It is important then to answer the question as to why the child was given up in terms of the situation rather than in emotionally coloured terms, in other words to point out explicitly the difficult circumstances the mother was likely to be in. This does not have to be far from the truth, for with most parents who give up their child it is the circumstances which instigate the giving up rather than indifference or a lack of love for the child.

In any case, it is certain that the overall upbringing in the adoptive family is of great significance for the way the child will deal with his background. If there is a sound relation between the child and the adoptive parents or, in terms of the beginning of this chapter, a sound psychological parenthood has evolved, knowledge about the biological parents will be of less importance for the personal identity development and the build-up of a positive and stable self-image than when this relation is less successful. Because the self-image is sufficiently stable already, any possible information about the background will hardly change this. One should, however, meet any realistic curiosity by adoptive children in connection with this as positively as possible. After all, Triseliotis discovered that the need for information is related to the amount of information already available. As adoptees had more information at their disposal, the need for even more information decreased. However, even more interesting is that Triseliotis, as well as Jaffee and Fanshel, found a connection between the quality of relations in the adoptive family and the nature of the desired information. The worse the mutual relations in the family, the stronger the desire to meet the biological parents. The few adoptees who, after searching for a long time, eventually found the parents or other close relatives more often than not had a disappointing experience. For example, an eighteen-year-old boy reported: 'My first father lives in the Netherlands and I have met him once, but he remains a stranger to me'. After that, however, he found it much easier to reconcile himself to the situation.

It should be noted that the reaction of a parent who has once given up a child is greatly influenced by the situation at the time the child was conceived and the reactions that were then given by the social environment, especially the regard in which giving up a child is held in that country. General remarks cannot be made in this context, except, perhaps, this one: to many birth mothers the fact of giving up a child has a strong influence on the rest of their lives. The day of birth will only rarely be forgotten; perhaps it will be suppressed. Sometimes the birth parents themselves go searching for the child they gave up ten, twenty, perhaps thirty years before. Just how the adoptee will be approached then depends on many circumstances, but it does not always have to be disappointing, nor will they immediately 'hit it off'. It does happen that, after several positive conversations, the interest of the adoptee or the parent slowly drains away; the novelty has worn off, one's curiosity has been satisfied. Bear in mind that the expectations and the reactions of both parties may differ a great deal. To the birth mother, the birth and the giving up of the child may be a trauma that has not been dealt with, while for the adoptee in question, the reason for the quest is principally curiosity about his genealogy. This curiosity, or the strong need for at least one meeting, may also lead to searches at a much later age, or even after the adoptive parents have died.

In the study it has been questioned whether the adoptive parents have the impression that the children sometimes think about their adoptive parents. This is the case for almost half of the parents. However, in children older than twelve, this is 75 per cent. During puberty it will often be found that the adolescent is more or less intensively occupied with his natural parents. This has to do with his identity development and his approaching adulthood. Many parents ask themselves if the lack of information will give rise to problems, especially during puberty. Of the greatest importance – as it turned out – is the relationship between parents and children and the willingness of parents to make available as much information as possible, including the personal adoption documents. It will probably help if the adoptee has at least some knowledge about his country of origin. In this manner, part of the curiosity can be satisfied rationally. In order to be of help with this, we have listed a number of informative books about several major adoptive countries in the appendices. Increasingly, queries are made from the country of origin. In some cases this may lead to a correspondence between the birth parents and the adoptive parents or the adoptee. Gradually, a lot of experience has been gained through these contacts. The most important conclusion from this is that, especially at first, it is best that these contacts run through official channels, often the intermediate institution. The iron law of secrecy can no longer be maintained in any case. An adoptee is entitled to information concerning his genetic background and parents who have given up their child should not be denied the right to receive information about that child.

To Conclude

When in all countries in post-war Europe the legislation which arranged the adoption of children eventually came into effect, it was not foreseen that these adoption laws would be applicable to entirely different children and different families. Neither did people realise how complicated and comprehensive the world of adoption was. With the arrival of children from the Third World, and also with the changed views of what is in the best interest of the child, the picture has thoroughly changed since 1970.

Families who have adopted children from Colombia, India, Sri Lanka, Brazil, Romania and a further thirty-odd countries, are faced with different problems than families which had adopted a child before. Then, it was almost always a small baby of the same race and, usually, of a young unmarried mother who lived in the same country. The latter group of children has dropped to less than five per one million inhabitants in countries like Sweden, the Netherlands, Belgium, France and other European countries. To put it another way, the number of children given up each year is less than forty per 100,000 births – a figure which is by no means sufficient for the increased interest in adoption from couples who cannot have children themselves or already have one or more natural children.

What has remained are the high expectations, the good-will and the great effort of adoptive parents. These characteristics of adoptive families are absolutely necessary, but not enough, to make all adoptions a success. A lot more is needed in many adoptions of foreign children of a different race who were often neglected, abused and in bad physical condition when they arrived.

In the preceding chapters, I have given a great deal of information about various behavioural problems with these children when they have just been taken into the family and later, during puberty. This information can help parents to fulfil their task as educators as much as possible and to actually see the education as a task where one accepts that a good result cannot be taken for granted.

But, let me again repeat it explicitly, a basic condition for all adoptions is that the educator loves children, dearly likes to raise children and is completely devoted to this. When this attitude is combined with realistic expectations, a certain distance with regard to one's own emotions and those of the child, lots of patience, flexibility with regard to fixed convictions about education and some knowledge about the influences of problematic experiences on the behaviour of children, the chances of the adoption being a success for all parties involved will be considerably larger.

I have written this book with this goal in mind, and with the knowledge that the way in which foreign children are placed still leaves a lot to be desired from a psychological and pedagogical point of view.

I hope that the tens of thousands of young children who are, willy-nilly, moved far from their country of birth every year will regard their new country and new home as their *home*.

References

Allport, G.W. (1954) *The Nature of Prejudice.* Cambridge, MA: Addison-Weshly.

Bachrach, C.A., Adams, P.F., Sambrano, S. and London, K.A. (1990) 'Adoption in the 1980s.' *Advance Data from Vital and Health Statistics of the National Center for Health Statistics 181,* 5 January 1990.

Banks, N. (1992) 'Techniques for direct identity work with Black children.' *British Agencies for Adoption and Fostering 16,* 3, 19–25.

Dale, D. (1987) *Denying Homes to Black Children: Britain's New Race Adoption Policies. Research Report 8.* London: Social Affairs Unit.

DSM-III-R (1987) *Diagnostic and Statistical Manual of Disorders.* Washington DC: American Psychiatric Association.

Egmond, G. van (1987) *Bodemloos bestaan. Problemen met adoptiekinderen (Bottomless existence. Problems with adoptive children).* Baarn: Ambo.

Fischer, A. (1973) *In Search for Anna Fischer.* New York: Arthur Fields.

Flango, V.E. and Flango, C.R. (1995) New York, NY: Child Welfare League of America.

Foreign Adoption (1–10–1987) *Why did you abandon me?* Bombay: Indian Association for Promotion of Adoption.

Gardell, I. (1980) *A Swedish Study on Intercountry Adoptions.* Stockholm: Liber Tryck.

Geerars, H.C., 't Hart, H. and Hoksbergen, R.A.C. (1991) *Waar ben ik thuis? Geadopteerde adolescenten over adoptie, hun familie, problemen, uithuisplaatsing en toekomstvisie (Where am I at home? Adopted adolescents about adoption, their family, problems, out-placement, and future outlook).* Utrecht: Adoption Centre.

Grow, L.J. and Shapiro, D. (1975) *Transracial Adoption Today.* New York, NY: Child Welfare League of America.

Hall, T. (1986) 'The adoption revolution in Britain.' In R.A.C. Hoksbergen and S.D. Gokhale (eds) *Adoption in Worldwide Perspective.* Berwyn: Swets North America Inc.

Hart-de Ruijter, T. and Kamp, L.N.J. (1972) *Hoofdlijnen van de kinderpsychiatrie* (Main subjects of child psychiatry). Deventer: Van Loghum Slaterus.

Hoksbergen, R.A.C. (1991), Bunjes, L., Baarda, B. and Nota, J. (1982) *Adoptie van kinderen uit verre landen (Adoption of children from far countries).* Deventer: Van Loghum Slaterus.

Hoksbergen, R.A.C. (1983) 'Adoptiefkinderen bij Medisch Opvoedkundige Bureaus (MOB) en Jeugdpsychiatrische Diensten (JPD)' (Adoptive children at institutes for public health). In R.A.C. Hoksbergen and H. Walenkamp *Adoptie uit de kinderschoenen (Adoption out of infancy)*. Deventer: Van Loghum Slaterus.

Hoksbergen, R.A.C., Juffer, F. and Waardenburg, B.C. (1986) *Adoptiekinderen thuis en op school (Adoptive children at home and at school). The adjustment after eight years of 116 Thai children in the Dutch community*. Lisse: Swets and Zeitlinger.

Hoksbergen, R.A.C., Spaan, J.J.T.M. and Waardenburg, B.C. (1988) *Bittere ervaringen (Bitter experiences)*. Lisse: Swets and Zeitlinger.

Hoksbergen, R.A.C. and Walenkamp, H. (1991) *Kind van andere ouders. Theorie en praktijk van adoptie (Child of Other Parents. Theory and Practice of Adoption)*. Houten: Bohn Stafleu Van Loghum

ICODO INFO (1992) *Themanummer: Joodse onderduikkinderen van toen (Thesis: Jewish children be in hiding, then)*. Utrecht: Stichting ICODO, 9e jrg. nr. 92–2.

Jaffee, B. and Fanshel, D. (1970) *How They Fared in Adoption*. New York: Colombia University Press.

Juffer, F. (1993) *Verbonden door adoptie. Een experimentele onderzoek naar hechting en competentie in gezinnen met een adoptiebaby (Bound by adoption. An experimental study of attachment and competence in families with an adoptive baby)*. Amersfoort: ACCO.

Juffer, F. (1988) *Ik ben Shira. Ik ben geadopteerd (I am Shira, I am adopted)*. Utrecht: Adoptie Centrum, Universiteit Utrecht.

Keilson, H. (1979) *Sequentielle Traumatisierung bei Kindern. Deskriptiv-klinische und quantifizierend-statistische follow-up Untersuchung zum Schicksal der jüdischen Kriegswaisen in den Niederlanden*. Stuttgart: Ferdinand Enke Verlag.

Kirk, H.D. (1981) *Adoptive kinship. A Modern Institution in Need of Reform*. Toronto: Butterworths.

Krech, D., Crutchfield, R.S. and Ballachey, E.L. (1962) *Individual in Society. A Textbook of Social Psychology*. New York: McGraw-Hill Book Company, Inc. and Chuster.

Lifton, B.J. (1975) *Twice Born: Memoirs of an Adopted Daughter*. New York: McGraw-Hill.

Lifton, B.J. (1979) *Lost and Found. The Adoption Experience*. New York: The Dial Press.

Lythcott-Haims, J.C. (1994) 'Where do mixed babies belong? Racial classification in America and its implications for transracial adoption.' *Harvard Civil Rights-Civil Liberties Law Review 29*, 531–558.

O'Brian, C. (1994) 'Transracial adoption in Hong Kong.' *Child Welfare LXXIII*, 4 July/August, 319–331.

Paton, J.M. (1954) *The Adopted Break Silence*. Philadelphia, PA: Life History Study Center.

Pierce, W. and Vitillo, R.J. (1991) 'Independent adoptions and the "Baby Market".' In E.D. Hibbs (ed) *Adoption, International Perspectives*. Madison/Connecticut: International Universities Press.

Ramondt, S. (1984) *Mythen en sagen van de Griekse wereld (Myths and legends from the Greek World)*. Weesp: Fibula van Dishoeck.

Sorgedrager, N. (1988) *Oriënterend medisch onderzoek en groeistudie van buitenlandse adoptiekinderen (Medical examination and growth of foreign born adoptive children)*. Haren: Cicero.

Sorosky, A.D., Baran, A. and Pannor, R. (1984) *Adoption Triangle*. New York: Anchor Books.

Tahk, Y.T. (1986) 'Inter-country adoption program in Korea.' In R.A.C. Hoksbergen. *Adoption in Worldwide Perspective. A Review of Programs, Policies and Legislation in 14 Countries*. Lisse: Swets and Zeitlinger, BV.

Triseliotis, J. (1973) *In Search of Origins. The Experiences of Adopted People*. London: Routledge and Kegan Paul.

Trouw (1988) 'Maricella praat alleen in gedachten met haar ouders' (Maricella talks with her biological parents only in private). *Trouw*.

Velde te, E.R. (1991) *Zwanger worden in de 21ste eeuw: steeds later, steeds kunstmatiger (Becoming pregnant in the 21st century: constantly later, constantly more artificial)*. Utrecht: Universiteit Utrecht oratie.

Verhulst, F.C. and Versluis-den Bieman, H.J.M. (1989) *Buitenlandse adoptiekinderen: vaardigheden en probleemgedrag (Foreign adoptees: competences and problem behaviour)*. Assen/Maastricht: Van Gorcum.

Verrier, N.N. (1993) *The Primal Wound*. Baltimore: Gateway Press, Inc.

Vries de, A.K. (1987) *Een nieuwe start...een nieuwe taal (A new start...a new language)*. Utrecht: Brochure van het Adoptie Centrum, Universiteit Utrecht.

Winick, M., Meyer, K.K. and Harris, R.C. (1976) 'Malnutrition and environmental enrichment by early adoption.' *Science*, 19th December, 1173–1175.

Witte de, H.F.J. (1990) 'Ontwikkelingspsychopathie en Psychopathiforme Gedragsstoornissen (Conduct Disorders).' In J.A.R. Sanders-Woudstra and H.F.J. Witte de (eds) *Leerboek Kinderen Jeugdpsychiatrie*. Assen: Van Gorcum.

Further Reading

Austin, J. (ed) (1985) *Adoption: The Inside Story.* Barn Owl Books

Chennells, P. and Hammond, C. (1995) *Adopting a Child: A Guide for People Interested in Adoption.* London: British Agencies for Adoption and Fostering.

Harris, K. (1985) *Transracial Adoption: A Bibliography.* London: British Agencies for Adoption and Fostering.

Howe, D. (1996) *Adopters on Adoption: Reflections on Parenthood and Children.* London: British Agencies for Adoption and Fostering.

Kay, J. (1991) *The Adoption Papers.* Newcastle: Bloodaxe Books.

Lambert, L., Buist, M., Triseliotis, J. and Hill, M. (1990) *Freeing Children for Adoption.* London: British Agencies for Adoption and Fostering.

Sparks, K. (1995) *Why Adoption?* London: British Agencies for Adoption and Fostering and Thomas Coram Foundation.

Triseliotis, J. (1988) (ed) *Groupwork in Adoption and Foster Care.* London: British Agencies for Adoption and Fostering and Batsford.

Wells, S. (1995) *Within Me, Without Me: Adoption – An Open and Shut Case?* London: Scarlet Press

Brochure of the Adoption Centre

Adoption

Adoption as a real situation of bringing-up is probably as old as mankind. The fact that parents cannot take care of their offspring is something that has occurred for centuries. Sometimes because the parents simply died early; sometimes because of unintentionally losing sight of one another, through war, natural disasters, or shortage of food. However, sometimes the child can be absolutely unwanted by the natural parents.

The Romans established the legal bond between the person to be adopted and the adopting parents. Especially in cases of childlessness, the father would adopt a child in order to have an heir to inherit the heritage. Through the rise of Christianity, legal adoption fell into disuse. This was also the case in the Netherlands. When, for instance, in 1838 the Civil Code was introduced, there was no legal provision for adoption because 'no human establishment can create relations that are not based on nature' and 'adoption is in defiance of our national character'.

The developments of the past decades prove how wrong the last statement was. On 26 January 1956, after extensive preparations and delay by World War II, the adoption law came into effect. In the Netherlands today (1994), there are approximately 25,000 adoptees of Dutch origin (step-parents included) and approximately 20,000 adoptees of foreign descent. Every year approximately 800 foreign adopted children are added to this number.

Research and education

Adoption as a social phenomenon has gained solid ground, but the newness of it did of course raise many questions. Since the 1970s, researchers at the University of Utrecht have been intensely engaged in adoption research and education. In 1984 the present Adoption Centre was founded. The Adoption Centre is a part of the large study group Youth, Family and the Life Development (JGL) of the Faculty of Social Sciences. Research is done on the adjustment of adoption children originating from different countries, on the attachment of adopted children to their new parents and on the causes of difficulties in the process of placements. Likewise, research is done on the experience of being adopted and on the factors that contribute to the cases in which the children are having psychological and emotional problems in their adoption families. The aspect of 'openness' regarding the origin and background of the child is one of the subjects of research.

About 60 students from different universities and studies apply for courses on adoption and related phenomena each year. This interest also encourages many of the Adoption Centre's research activities. On 5 December 1984 we were able to fill the professorial chair of adoption. On 28 May 1993, Femmie Juffer was awarded her Ph.D for her thesis *Joined together by Adoption*. More theses will follow.

Information and consultation

Many people, departments, and organisations are involved with adoption. One can think of the 19 Boards for Child Protection, the 11 adoption (mediation) organisations, all welfare agencies, and of course, especially, the many adoption families in our country. But many lines can also be drawn from abroad to Dutch families. Staff at the Adoption Centre consider themselves fortunate in being given the opportunity, by the University of Utrecht, to meet the many different needs for education, information, and consultation. This is done through lectures, production of films and brochures, reporting on specific subjects, being part of committees, functioning as advisers and through personal contacts with different people asking for information and some sort of psychological assistance.

In January 1989 we founded our Documentation Centre. Two people assemble new articles and books on the subject of adoption/non-genetic parenthood. All received literature will be read and computerised. Since January 1990 we have also published the magazine *Adoption/Non-Genetic Parenthood*. We do this together with four other organisations working in the field of adoption.

Educational assistance

Experience has shown that adoption can go hand-in-hand with specific educational problems. The fact that every adoptee has two sets of parents is not without difficulties for both child and parents. In the growth towards adulthood, and the connected identity development, the child may struggle with specific problems. For foreign children the influences of racial differences can be added to these problems. Some children may experience long-lasting serious consequences of physical and emotional neglect during the first months or years of their existence. Adoption parents usually have specific questions. They gratefully ask advice from people with experience in this field, often other adoption parents. At other times they contact the Adoption Centre for advice. The central location of the Adoption Centre, in Utrecht, makes this easy. Evidently, where possible, one is sent to a local social service. A broad network of contacts has already been built up through social workers, specialists in child care, and employed by the Ambulatorium of our Faculty of Social Sciences.

Material resources

The Adoption Centre receives financial support from several adoption organisations. Grants are also given for research projects, documentation, and secretarial assistance. The most important material support is obtained from funds of the University of Utrecht.

Publications

Hoksbergen, R.A.C., Baarda, D.B., Bunjes, L.A.C. en Nota, J.A. (red.), (1979/1982). Adoptie van kinderen uit verre landen. Deventer: Van Loghum Slaterus. 235 pag. ƒ 25,00

Hoksbergen, R.A.C. en Walenkamp, H. (red.) (1980) Opgroeiende adoptiefkinderen. Deventer: Van Loghum Slaterus. 180 pag. ƒ 25,00

Hoksbergen, R.A.C. en Walenkamp, H. (red.) (1983/1985) Adoptie uit de kinderschoenen. Deventer: Van Loghum Slaterus. 342 pag. ƒ 25,00

Hoksbergen, R.A.C. en Gokhale, S.D. (red.) (1986) Adoption in Worldwide Perspective. Lisse: Swets and Zeitlinger. 242 pag. ƒ 38,00

Hoksbergen, R.A.C., Juffer, F. en Waardenburg, B.C. (1986) Adoptiekinderen thuis en op school. Lisse: Swets and Zeitlinger. 136 pag. ƒ 19,50

Hoksbergen, R.A.C., Juffer, F. en Waardenburg, B.C. (1987) Adopted Children at Home and at School. Lisse: Swets and Zeitlinger. 105 pag. ƒ 10,00

Hoksbergen, R.A.C., Meer, R. van der en Schoon, G.P. (red.) (1987) Adolescenten in vele gedaanten. Lisse: Swets and Zeitlinger. 207 pag. ƒ 30,00

Juffer, F. (1988) Ik ben Shira. Ik ben geadopteerd. Utrecht: Adoptie Centrum. 37 pag. ƒ 12,00

Hoksbergen, R.A.C., Spaan, J.J.Th.M. en Waardenburg, B.C. (1988/1991) Bittere ervaringen. Utrecht: Adoptie Centrum. 120 pag. ƒ 20,00

Vries, A.K. de en Bunjes, L.A.C. (1989) Een nieuwe start...een nieuwe taal. Utrecht: Adoptie Centrum. 84 pag. ƒ 12,50

Hoksbergen, R.A.C. en Wolters, W.H.G. (red.) (1989) Verstoorde relaties – adoptie en hulpverlening. Baarn: Ambo. 127 pag. ƒ 20,00

Hoksbergen, R.A.C. en Bunjes, L.A.C. (1989) Een buitenlands kind adopteren – gids voor adoptie-ouders en hun begeleiders. Amersfoort: ACCO. 105 pag. ƒ. 19,90

Hoksbergen R.A.C. en Steenkiste, B. van. (1991) Adoptie van een kind in Vlaanderen. Utrecht: Adoptie Centrum. 70 pag. ƒ 12,50

Juffer, F. (1991) Wat betekent het om een buitenlands kind te adopteren? Utrecht: Adoptie Centrum. 21 pag. ƒ 5,00

Vries, A.K. de en Rooda, J.M. (1991) Adoptiekinderen uit Mauritius. Utrecht: Adoptie Centrum. 41 pag. ƒ 10,00

Hoksbergen, R.A.C. en Walenkamp, H. (red.) (1991) Kind van andere ouders. Houten: Bohn Stafleu Van Loghum. 304 pag. ƒ 50,00

Geerars, H.C., Hart, H. 't en Hoksbergen, R.A.C. (1991) Waar ben ik thuis? Utrecht: Adoptie Centrum. 150 pag. ƒ 22,50

Brouwer-Van Dalen C. (1992 – 1993) Landen informatie; Ethiopië, Taiwan, China, Colombia. Utrecht: Adoptie Centrum. ƒ 17,50 per uitgave

Hoksbergen, R.A.C. en Textor, M.R. (red.) (1993) Adoption. Grundlagen, Vermittlung, Nachbetreuung, Beratung. Freiburg: Lambertus. 251 pag. ƒ 39,50

Juffer, F. (1993) Verbonden door adoptie. Een experimenteel onderzoek naar hechting en competentie in gezinnen met een adoptiebaby. Amersfoort: Acco. 254 pag. ƒ 44,00

Hoksbergen, R.A.C. (1994) Een kind adopteren. Gids voor adoptieouders en hun raadgevers. Baarn: Ambo. 144 pag. ƒ 30,00

Rosenboom, L.G. (1994) Gemengde gezinnen, gemengde gevoelens? Hechting en competentie van adoptiebaby's in gezinnen met biologisch eigen kinderen. Utrecht: Universiteit Utrecht, Adoptie Centrum. 181 pag. ƒ 30,00

Hoksbergen, R.A.C. (red.) (1994) Met het oog op adoptie. Lezingen conferentie 4 juni 1994 en toonaangevende artikelen 1984–1994 over adoptie, Niet-genetisch ouderschap. Utrecht: Universiteit Utrecht, Adoptie Centrum. 314 pag. ƒ 39,00

Geerars, H.C., Hoksbergen R.A.C. and Rooda, J. (1995) Geadopteerden op weg naar volwassenheid. De integratie van 68 Thaise jongeren in de Nederlandse samenleving. Utrecht: Universiteit Utrecht, Adoptie Centrum. 210 pag. ƒ 30,00

Geerars, H.C., Hoksbergen, R.A.C. and Rooda, J. (1996) *Adoptees on their way to adulthood. The Integration of 68 Thai adoptees into Dutch Society.* Utrecht: Utrecht University Adoption Centre.

Hoksbergen, R.A.C., Storsbergen, H.E., Brouwer-van Dalen, C. (1995) Het begon in Griekenland. Een verkenning van de achtergrond van in Griekenland geboren, geadopteerde jongvolwassenen en de betekenis van de adoptiestatus. Utrecht: Universiteit Utrecht, Adoptie Centrum. 280 pag. ƒ 40,00

Hoksbergen, R.A.C. (1995). Hoe ver gaan we. Moderne voortplanting in feitelijk en ethisch perspectief. Baarn: Ambo. 207 pag. ƒ 39,90

Videotapes

Adoptie uit de Kinderschoenen. (Adoption coming of age).

Natuurlijk blijf je anders. (Naturally you remain different).

Both videotapes are English subtitled.

These publications can be purchased at the Adoption Centre.

Documentation Centre
    Visit: by appointment
    Open: Tuesday and Friday
    tel. 30 – 2534702

Adoption Centre
Universiteit Utrecht
Faculteit Sociale Wetenschappen
Vakgroep Jeugd, Gezin en Levensloop
Heidelberglaan 1
3584 CS Utrecht
The Netherlands
tel: 30 – 2534804
fax: 30 – 2531619
E-mail: adoptie@fsw.ruu.nl

Subject Index

Jessica Kingsley *Publishers*
116 Pentonville Road, London N1 9JB

Author Index

Raising Responsible Teenagers

Bob Myers
ISBN 1 85302 429 5 pb

Raising Responsible Teenagers combines comprehensive discussion about child development with practical advice on parenting styles and discipline techniques. Each stage of child development is discussed, creating a picture of childhood, the springboard to adult life and a time where the child 'is at' on entering adolescence. Adolescence is blended into a mixture that parents can still greatly influence, such as the usefulness of

Bob Myers provides the tools for this, such as the usefulness agreed on by all the family and based on the simple principles and safety for everyone'. Being a realist, he also offers behaviour and shows how adults in the parenting their own parenting skills, rather than focusing contains useful examples and checklists for of useful advice.

This book will provide an extremely all those who wish to interact with your and who wish to see them become c

challenging behaviour
to these difficult behaviours ha

Author Index

Parenting Teenagers

Bob Myers

ISBN 1 85302 366 3 pb

'...a most enjoyable read. Thankfully, it is not aimed at your 2.3 kids nuclear family but it is also inclusive of separated families, single parents, residential workers, social workers etc. There is something for everyone in this book. This is a book I will use in my work with parents and carers alike.'

— Irish Social Worker

'...an easy to read, practical guide to parenting teenagers. It covers a number of areas including communication, the move from teenager to adulthood, 'letting go of your teenager', explanations for teenager misbehaviour with practical suggestions on how to cope with it, and how the parent teenager relationship can be strengthened. The book discusses the physical, emotional and psychological changes experienced at adolescence, and how parental skills can be adapted to cope with these changes.'

— Talk: Magazine of the National Deaf Children's Society

'...a friendly, useful book for concerned parents... [Myers] emphasises consistency and continuity in responding to other people, and exhorts how control and patience in relation to ourselves, and being able to think inventively about our sons and daughters, can result in more positive and equal relationships... Myers offers a supportive and sensible voice to parents, and suggests that patient use of the right strategies will bring positive results in the end.'

— Young Minds Magazine

'It was again reassuring to read that many of the more disturbing phases of the teens are not unusual, just maddening... I am sure that I will draw on the ideas I have read in my professional conversations with parents and young people.'

Bob Myers has, since 1979, been Director of the Brophy Memorial Hostel, where he works with young people who are either homeless or unable to live at home. Some have been severely emotionally damaged and present very challenging behaviours. Bob has adopted the radical approach that solutions to these difficult behaviours have to be found, without the option of expulsion.

Jessica Kingsley *Publishers*
116 Pentonville Road, London N1 9JB

Raising Responsible Teenagers

Bob Myers

ISBN 1 85302 429 5 pb

Raising Responsible Teenagers combines comprehensive discussion about child development with practical advice on parenting styles and discipline techniques. Each stage of child development is discussed, creating a picture of where the child 'is at' on entering adolescence. Adolescence is the final stage of childhood, the springboard to adult life and a time where values are being blended into a mixture that parents can still greatly influence.

Bob Myers provides the tools for this, such as the use of rules made and agreed on by all the family and based on the simple philosophy of 'a fair go and safety for everyone'. Being a realist, he also offers ways of handling difficult behaviour and shows how adults in the parenting role can focus control on their own parenting skills, rather than focusing just on the child. Each chapter contains useful examples and checklists for further thought, as well as a fund of useful advice.

This book will provide an extremely useful guide for parents, teachers and all those who wish to interact with young people in a conflict-free atmosphere, and who wish to see them become considerate, achieving and responsible adults.

Jessica Kingsley *Publishers*
116 Pentonville Road, London N1 9JB

Play Therapy
Where the Sky Meets the Underworld
Ann Cattanach

ISBN 1 85302 211 X pb

'...an excellent, stimulating read with a manageable style and numerous sensitive insights into the world of play for the child and how it can become a therapeutic process where children 'play out' their perception of their own experiences...uses clear, straightforward language to discuss the theoretical basis for play therapy... The book does not make great claims as to its powers of healing, but it seems to offer a means towards constructively working through traumatic experiences for children.' -- *Nursery World*

'Cattanach packs a large amount of theory into this easy-to-read volume, together with practical guidelines on how to be a safe companion for the child's journey.' -- *Professional Social Work*

'This is an excellent introduction to an activity whose relevance is increasingly recognised and used, not least in the communication of good health practices.'

-- Institute of Health Education

'This is a short and accessible work on a subject of considerable interest to many professionals... Cattanach uses the language of imagination and myth, rather than the more mundane style we have come to expect in works about therapy and teaching. However, she uses it with authority as an international expert.'

-- Child Language Teaching and Therapy

Ann Cattanach MSc, CSTD, RDTh, is Course Director, Play Therapy at Roehampton Institute and is co-founder of The Play Therapy Trust. She helped to develop the Dramatherapy course at the Akademie de Kopese Hof, Nijmegen, Netherlands and supervises the Play Therapy course in Athens run by the Centre for Dramatherapy, Theatre and Therapy. She works as a therapist for Harrow NHS Community Trust and acts as a Child Care Consultant/Therapist for several Social Service departments in London. She is the author of several books, including *Play Therapy with Abused Children* published in 1992 by Jessica Kingsley Publishers.

Jessica Kingsley *Publishers*
116 Pentonville Road, London N1 9JB

Emotional Milestones
from Birth to Adulthood
A Psychodynamic Approach
Ruth Schmidt Neven

ISBN 1 85302 456 2 pb

Emotional Milestones offers parents, carers and teachers a conceptual frame-work for understanding and facilitating child and family development. The psychodynamic approach combines theoretical understanding and practical observation to create a new way of understanding human behaviour which can influence the way we organise services and facilities for children and parents. Key concepts in this approach include:

- all behaviour has meaning and is always a communication between children and adults
- understanding a child's 'problem' behaviour in this way opens up communication
- behaviour is dynamic and changes all the time
- our inner world of dreams, fantasy and play is important in the construction of self
- the need to understand the child as an individual and within the context of the family
- the provision of 'containment' for children.

Emotional Milestones is a thought-provoking book which offers an exciting new model for the type of parents and carers we can become.

Ruth Schmidt Neven trained as a child psychotherapist at the Tavistock Clinic in London, became the first Chief Child Psychotherapist at the Royal Children's Hospital in Melbourne, established the Centre for Child and Family Development in Melbourne in 1994 and writes and lectures extensively on child development.

Jessica Kingsley *Publishers*
116 Pentonville Road, London N1 9JB